Bell's Latin Course for the First Year in Three Parts, Volume 3 – Primary Source Edition

Edgar Cardew Marchant, J G. Spencer

BELL'S LATIN COURSE

PART III

RDF

BELL'S LATIN COURSE

FOR THE FIRST YEAR

IN THREE PARTS

BY

E. C. MARCHANT, M.A.

AND

J. G. SPENCER, B.A.

ASSISTANT MASTER AT ST. PAUL'S PREPARATORY SCHOOL

PART III

LONDON: GEORGE BELL & SONS
YORK STREET, COVENT GARDEN
1901

Oxford

HORACE HART, PRINTER TO THE UNIVERSITY

CONTENTS

———•———

LIST OF ILLUSTRATIONS

SUMMARY OF GRAMMAR

IN

PARTS I AND II

———+·+———

FIRST DECLENSION.

Sing.		*Plur.*
Nom.	Aquil-a, an eagle.	Aquil-ae, eagles.
Acc.	Aquil-am, an eagle.	Aquil-ās, eagles.
Gen.	Aquil-ae, of an eagle.	Aquil-ārum, of eagles.
Dat.	Aquil-ae, to *or* for an eagle.	Aquil-īs, to *or* for eagles.
Abl.	Aquil-ā, by, with *or* from an eagle.	Aquil-īs, by, with *or* from eagles.

NOTE I. Substantives of the first declension are **feminine** except those denoting males ; as, **agricola**, 'a farmer'; **nauta**, 'a sailor.'

NOTE II. A few feminine substantives have -**ābus** in the dative and ablative plural to distinguish them from the corresponding cases of masculine substantives in the second declension ; as, de-**ābus** and fīli-**ābus**.

SECOND DECLENSION.

MASCULINE SUBSTANTIVES IN -US.

Sing.		*Plur.*
Nom.	Domin-us, a lord.	Domin-ī, lords.
Voc.	Domin-e, O lord.	Domin-ī, O lords.
Acc.	Domin-um, a lord.	Domin-ōs, lords.
Gen.	Domin-ī, of a lord.	Domin-ōrum, of lords.
Dat.	Domin-ō, to *or* for a lord.	Domin-īs, to *or* for lords.
Abl.	Domin-ō, by, with *or* from a lord.	Domin-īs, by, with *or* from lords.

Vocative Form. A few substantives ending in -us in the nominative have a vocative form in -e, which is used in addressing an object. In all other substantives the nominative and vocative forms are the same.

MASCULINE SUBSTANTIVES IN -ER.

Puer, masc., 'A Boy.'   Magister, masc., 'A Master.'

	Sing.	Plur.
Nom.	Puer	Puer-ī
Acc.	Puer-um	Puer-ōs
Gen.	Puer-ī	Puer-ōrum
Dat.	Puer-ō	Puer-īs
Abl.	Puer-ō	Puer-īs.

Most substantives, however, in -er drop the e in all other cases; as, magister, magistrum (not magisterum).

NEUTER SUBSTANTIVES IN -UM.

Bellum, neut., 'War.'

	Sing.	Plur.
Nom., Acc.	Bell-um	Bell-a
Gen.	Bell-ī	Bell-ōrum
Dat., Abl.	Bell-ō	Bell-īs.

Note I.   Substantives ending in -us and -er are masculine; those in -um are neuter.

Note II.   Substantives ending in -ius have the vocative singular in -ī; as, fīlī, 'O son'; Claudī, 'O Claudius,' and in the genitive singular ii is often contracted into ī, as Claudī, ' of Claudius.'

Note III.   Deus, 'a god,' usually has a contracted form dī in nominative plural, and dīs, in dative and ablative plural, and sometimes deum in genitive plural.

THIRD DECLENSION.

IMPARISYLLABIC SUBSTANTIVES.

MASCULINE SUBSTANTIVES IN -Ŏ, -OR, -ŌS, -ER, -ES, -EX.

Leo, 'A Lion.'   Stem LEŌN-.

	Sing.	Plur.
Nom.	Leō	Leōn-ēs
Acc.	Leōn-em	Leōn-ēs
Gen.	Leōn-is	Leōn-um
Dat.	Leōn-i	Leōn-ibus
Abl.	Leōn-e	Leōn-ibus.

Victor, *gen.* Victōr-is, 'A Conqueror'; *Stem* Victōr-.
Honōs, *gen.* Honōr-is, 'Honour'; *Stem* Honōr-.
Carcer, *gen.* Carcer-is, 'A Prison'; *Stem* Carcer-.
Mīles, *gen.* Mīlit-is, 'A Soldier'; *Stem* Mīlit-.
Iūdex, *gen.* Iūdic-is, 'A Judge'; *Stem* Iūdic-.

Monosyllables with Stem ending in Single Consonant.

Flōs, *gen.* Flōr-is, 'A Flower'; *Stem* Flōr-.
Pēs, *gen.* Ped-is, 'A Foot'; *Stem* Ped-.
Rex, *gen.* Rēg-is, 'A King'; *Stem* Rēg-.

FEMININE SUBSTANTIVES IN -ĀS, -DO, -GO, -IO AND -ŪS.

VIRGO, 'A MAIDEN.' Stem VIRGIN-.

	Sing.	*Plur.*
Nom.	Virgo	Virgin-ēs
Acc.	Virgin-em	Virgin-ēs
Gen.	Virgin-is	Virgin-um
Dat.	Virgin-i	Virgin-ibus
Abl.	Virgin-e	Virgin-ibus.

Multitūdo, *gen.* Multitūdin-is, 'A Multitude'; *Stem* Multitūdin-.
Legio, *gen.* Legiōn-is, 'A Legion'; *Stem* Legiōn-.
Honestās, *gen.* Honestāt-is, 'Honesty'; *Stem* Honestāt-.
Virtūs, *gen.* Virtūt-is, 'Virtue'; *Stem* Virtūt-.

NEUTER SUBSTANTIVES IN -UR, -US, -N AND -T.

CORPUS, gen. CORPOR-is, 'A BODY.' Stem CORPOR-.

	Sing.	*Plur.*
Nom., Acc.	Corpus	Corpor-a
Gen.	Corpor-is	Corpor-um
Dat.	Corpor-i	Corpor-ibus
Abl.	Corpor-e	Corpor-ibus.

Genus, *gen.* Gener-is, 'A Race'; *Stem* Gener-.
Ēbur, *gen.* Ēbor-is, 'Ivory'; *Stem* Ēbor-.
Nōmen, *gen.* Nōmin-is, 'A Name'; *Stem* Nōmin-.
Caput, *gen.* Capit-is, 'A Head'; *Stem* Capit-.

Monosyllables with Stem ending in Single Consonant.

	Sing.	*Plur.*
Nom., Acc.	Crūs	Crūr-a
Gen.	Crūr-is	Crūr-um
Dat.	Crūr-ī	Crūr-ibus
Abl.	Crūr-e	Crūr-ibus.

Similarly, Iūs, *gen.* Iūr-is, 'Law'; *Stem* Iūr-.

PARISYLLABIC SUBSTANTIVES.

MASCULINE SUBSTANTIVES IN -ER AND A FEW IN -IS.

IMBER, 'A SHOWER.' *Stem* IMBR-.

	Sing.	*Plur.*
Nom.	Imber	Imbr-ēs
Acc.	Imbr-em	Imbr-ēs
Gen.	Imbr-is	Imbr-ium
Dat.	Imbr-ī	Imbr-ibus
Abl.	Imbr-e	Imbr-ibus.

Orbis, *gen.* Orb-is, 'The World'; *Stem* Orb-.

FEMININE SUBSTANTIVES IN -ĒS AND -IS.

NŪBĒS, gen. NŪB-is, 'A CLOUD.' Stem NŪB-.

	Sing.	*Plur.*
Nom.	Nūb-ēs	Nūb-ēs
Acc.	Nūb-em	Nūb-ēs
Gen.	Nūb-is	Nūb-ium
Dat.	Nūb-i	Nūb-ibus
Abl.	Nūb-e	Nūb-ibus.

Ovis, *gen.* Ov-is, 'A Sheep'; *Stem* Ov-.

NEUTER SUBSTANTIVES IN -E, -AL, -AR.

MARE, gen. MAR-is, 'THE SEA.' Stem MAR-.

	Sing.	*Plur.*
Nom., Acc.	Mar-e	Mar-ia
Gen.	Mar-is	Mar-ium
Dat., Abl.	Mar-ī	Mar-ibus.

Animal, *gen.* Animāl-is, 'An Animal'; *Stem* Animāl-.
Calcar, *gen.* Calcār-is, 'A Spur'; *Stem* Calcār-.

Feminine Monosyllables with Stem ending in two Consonants.

URBS, gen. URB-is, 'A CITY.' Stem URB-.

	Sing.	*Plur.*
Nom.	Urbs	Urb-ēs
Acc.	Urb-em	Urb-ēs
Gen.	Urb-is	Urb-ium
Dat.	Urb-ī	Urb-ibus
Abl.	Urb-e	Urb-ibus.

Similarly, Arx, *gen.* Arc-is, 'Citadel'; Ars, *gen.* Art-is, 'Art';
Frons, *gen.* Front-is, 'Front'; Stirps, *gen.* Stirp-is, 'A Root'; the
Masculine Substantives As, *gen.* Ass-is, 'A Coin'; Dens, *gen.* Dent-is,
'A Tooth'; Mons, *gen.* Mont-is, 'Mountain'; Fons, *gen.* Font-is,
'Fountain'; Pons, *gen.* Pont-is, 'Bridge'; and the Neuter Os, *gen.*
Oss-is, 'A Bone.'

FOURTH DECLENSION.

MASCULINE SUBSTANTIVES IN -US.

PORTUS, gen. PORTŪ-s, 'A HARBOUR.' Stem PORTŪ-.

	Sing.	*Plur.*
Nom.	Portu-s	Portū-s
Acc.	Portu-m	Portū-s
Gen.	Portū-s	Portu-um
Dat.	Portu-ī	Port-ibus
Abl.	Portū	Port-ibus.

A few Substantives in -US are Feminine, as
Manus, *gen.* Manū-s, 'A Hand'; *Stem* Manū-.

NOTE.   A few words of two syllables in -cus and -tus usually have
-ubus in the dative and ablative plural; as, arcus, arcu-bus.
Domus, 'A House,' fem., has abl. sing. dom-ō, acc. plur. dom-ōs,
like the second declension.

NEUTER SUBSTANTIVES IN -U.

	Sing.	*Plur.*
Nom., Acc.	Genū	Genu-a
Gen.	Genū-s	Genu-um
Dat., Abl.	Genū	Gen-ibus.

FIFTH DECLENSION.

RĒS, gen. REĪ, fem. 'A THING.'

	Sing.	*Plur.*
Nom.	Rē-s	Rē-s
Acc.	Re-m	Rē-s
Gen.	Re-ī	Rē-rum
Dat.	Re-ī	Rē-bus
Abl.	Rē	Rē-bus.

DIĒS, gen. DIĒ-Ī, masc. 'A DAY.'

	Sing.	*Plur.*
Nom.	Diē-s	Diē-s
Acc.	Die-m	Diē-s
Gen.	Diē-ī	Diē-rum
Dat.	Diē-ī	Diē-bus
Abl.	Diē	Diē-bus.

NOTE. Dies is the only masculine substantive of this declension, though it is also feminine when it refers to 'an appointed day' or 'a period of time.' No other substantives of the declension are used in the genitive, dative, and ablative plural except dies and res.

ADJECTIVES IN -US, -A, -UM

Sing.

	M.	*F.*	*N.*
Nom.	Bon-us	Bon-a	Bon-um
Voc.	Bon-e	Bon-a	Bon-um
Acc.	Bon-um	Bon-am	Bon-um
Gen.	Bon-ī	Bon-ae	Bon-ī
Dat.	Bon-ō	Bon-ae	Bon-ō
Abl.	Bon-ō	Bon-ā	Bon-ō.

Plur.

	M.	*F.*	*N.*
Nom., Voc.	Bon-ī	Bon-ae	Bon-a
Acc.	Bon-ōs	Bon-ās	Bon-a
Gen.	Bon-ōrum	Bon-ārum	Bon-ōrum
Dat.	Bon-īs	Bon-īs	Bon-īs
Abl.	Bon-īs	Bon-īs	Bon-īs.

ADJECTIVES IN -ER, -ERA, -ERUM.

TENER, TENERA, TENERUM, 'TENDER.'

Sing.

	M.	*F.*	*N.*
Nom.	Tener	Tener-a	Tener-um
Acc.	Tener-um	Tener-am	Tener-um
Gen.	Tener-ī	Tener-ae	Tener-ī
Dat.	Tener-ō	Tener-ae	Tener-ō
Abl.	Tener-ō	Tener-a	Tener-ō.

The plural terminations are as in Bonus.

Many adjectives in -er drop the -e; as, Niger, nigra, nigrum, 'black.'

ADJECTIVES OF THE THIRD DECLENSION.

Trist-is, trist-e, 'Sad, gloomy.'

Two Terminations in Nominative Singular.

	Sing.		*Plur.*	
	M. and *F.*	*N.*	*M.* and *F.*	*N.*
Nom.	Trist-is	Trist-e	Trist-ēs	Trist-ia
Acc.	Trist-em	Trist-e	Trist-ēs	Trist-ia
Gen.	Trist-is	Trist-is	Trist-ium	Trist-ium
Dat.	Trist-ī	Trist-ī	Trist-ibus	Trist-ibus
Abl.	Trist-ī	Trist-ī	Trist-ibus	Trist-ibus.

Ācer, ācr-is, ācr-e, 'Keen.'

Three Terminations in Nominative Singular.

	Sing.			*Plur.*	
	M.	*F.*	*N.*	*M.* and *F.*	*N.*
Nom.	Ācer	Acr-is	Acr-e	Acr-ēs	Acr-ia
Acc.	Acr-em	Acr-em	Acr-e	Acr-ēs	Acr-ia
Gen.	Acr-is	Acr-is	Acr-is	Acr-ium	Acr-ium
Dat.	Acr-ī	Acr-ī	Acr-ī	Acr-ibus	Acr-ibus
Abl.	Acr-ī	Acr-ī	Acr-ī	Acr-ibus	Acr-ibus.

NOTE.   Celer, celer-is, celer-e keeps the e throughout before r in the stem.

Fēlix, fēlīc-is, 'Lucky, prosperous.'

One Termination in Nominative Singular.

	Sing.		*Plur.*	
	M. and *F.*	*N.*	*M.* and *F.*	*N.*
Nom.	Fēlix	Fēlix	Fēlīc-ēs	Fēlīc-ia
Acc.	Fēlīc-em	Fēlix	Fēlīc-ēs	Fēlīc-ia
Gen.	Fēlīc-is	Fēlīc-is	Fēlīc-ium	Fēlīc-ium
Dat.	Fēlīc-ī	Fēlīc-ī	Fēlīc-ibus	Fēlīc-ibus
Abl.	Fēlīc-ī *or* -e	Fēlīc-ī *or* -e	Fēlīc-ibus	Fēlīc-ibus.

PERSONAL PRONOUNS.

FIRST PERSON. Ego, 'I.'

Sing.				Plur.	
	Nom.	Ego			Nōs
	Acc.	Mē			Nōs
	Gen.	Meī			Nostrī *or* nostrum
	Dat.	Mihī			Nōbīs
	Abl.	Mē			Nōbīs.

SECOND PERSON. Tŭ, 'Thou *or* you.'

Sing.	*Nom.*	Tū	Plur.		Vōs
	Acc.	Tē			Vōs
	Gen.	Tuī			Vestrī *or* vestrum
	Dat.	Tibĭ			Vōbīs
	Abl.	Tē			Vōbīs.

NOTE ON GENITIVE CASE. The genitives mei, tui, nostri, vestri, are only used as objective genitives after adjectives like memor, 'mindful,' and cupidus, 'fond,' or substantives like timor, 'fear,' accusator, 'an accuser'; as, accusator mei, 'an accuser of me.'

The genitives nostrum and vestrum are only used as partitive genitives; as, multi nostrum, 'many of us'; unus vestrum, 'one of you.'

THE VERB ESSE, 'To Be.'

INDICATIVE MOOD.

		Present.	*Future Simple.*	*Imperfect.*
		I am.	I shall be.	I was.
Sing.	1.	Sum	Er-ŏ	Er-am
	2.	Es	Er-is	Er-ăs
	3.	Est	Er-it	Er-at
Plur.	1.	Sumus	Er-imus	Er-ămus
	2.	Estis	Er-itis	Er-ătis
	3.	Sunt	Er-unt	Er-ant.

		Perfect.	*Future Perfect.*	*Pluperfect.*
		I have been *or* I was.	I shall have been.	I had been.
Sing.	1.	Fu-ī	Fu-erō	Fu-eram
	2.	Fu-istī	Fu-eris	Fu-erăs
	3.	Fu-it	Fu-erit	Fu-erat
Plur.	1.	Fu-imus	Fu-erimus	Fu-erămus
	2.	Fu-istis	Fu-eritis	Fu-erătis
	3.	Fu-ērunt	Fu-erint	Fu-erant.

IMPERATIVE MOOD.

Present Tense.

Sing. 2. Es, 'Be thou.'   Plur. 2. Es-te, 'Be ye.'

NOTE. The compounds of sum (except possum) are inflected like sum; as, absum, 'I am absent'; adsum, 'I am present *or* at hand.'

FIRST CONJUGATION.

INDICATIVE MOOD.

AMĀ-RE, 'TO LOVE.' PRESENT STEM, AMĀ-.

		Present.	Future Simple.	Imperfect.
		I love.	I shall love.	I was loving.
Sing.	1.	Am-ō	Am-ābo	Am-ābam
	2.	Am-ās	Am-ābis	Am-ābās
	3.	Am-at	Am-ābit	Am-ābat
Plur.	1.	Am-āmus	Am-ābimus	Am-ābāmus
	2.	Am-ātis	Am-ābitis	Am-ābātis
	3.	Am-ant	Am-ābunt	Am-ābant.

PERFECT STEM. *amav*

		Perfect.	Future Perfect.	Pluperfect.
		I have loved *or* I loved.	I shall have loved.	I had loved.
Sing.	1.	Amāv-ī	Amāv-erō	Amāv-eram
	2.	Amāv-istī	Amāv-eris	Amāv-erās
	3.	Amāv-it	Amāv-erit	Amāv-erat
Plur.	1.	Amāv-imus	Amāv-erimus	Amāv-erāmus
	2.	Amāv-istis	Amāv-eritis	Amāv-erātis
	3.	Amāv-ērunt	Amāv-erint	Amāv-erant.

IMPERATIVE MOOD.

Present Tense.

Sing. 2. Amā, 'Love thou.'   Plur. 2. Amā-te, 'Love ye.'

THE VERB DO, 'I GIVE.'

The verb **do**, 'I give,' belongs to this conjugation, but has the a short in its present stem **da-** in all persons of the indicative except in the 2nd pers. sing. of the present tense.

Present. Do, dās, dăt, dămus, dătis, dant.
Future Simple. Dăbo.   *Imperfect.* Dăbam.

The perfect stem **ded-** is formed irregularly, but the endings are like those of amo.

Perfect. ded-i.   *Future Perfect.* ded-ero.   *Pluperfect.* ded-eram,

SECOND CONJUGATION.

INDICATIVE MOOD.

MONĒ-RE, 'TO ADVISE.' PRESENT STEM, MONĒ-.

	Present.	*Future Simple.*	*Imperfect.*
	I advise.	I shall advise.	I was advising.
Sing. 1.	Mon-eo	Mon-ēbo	Mon-ēbam
2.	Mon-ēs	Mon-ēbis	Mon-ēbās
3.	Mon-et	Mon-ēbit	Mon-ēbat
Plur. 1.	Mon-ēmus	Mon-ēbimus	Mon-ēbāmus
2.	Mon-ētis	Mon-ēbitis	Mon-ēbātis
3.	Mon-ent	Mon-ēbunt	Mon-ēbant.

PERFECT STEM, MONU-.

	Perfect.	*Future Perfect.*	*Pluperfect.*
	I have advised *or* I advised.	I shall have advised.	I had advised.
Sing. 1.	Monu-i	Monu-ero	Monu-eram
2.	Monu-isti	Monu-eris	Monu-erās
3.	Monu-it	Monu-erit	Monu-erat
Plur. 1.	Monu-imus	Monu-erimus	Monu-erāmus
2.	Monu-istis	Monu-eritis	Monu-erātis
3.	Monu-ērunt	Monu-erint	Monu-erant.

IMPERATIVE MOOD.

Present Tense.

Sing. 2. Mon-ē, 'Advise thou.' Plur. 2. Monē-te, 'Advise ye.'

THIRD CONJUGATION.

INDICATIVE MOOD.

REG-ERE, 'TO RULE.' PRESENT STEM, REG-.

	Present.	*Future Simple.*	*Imperfect.*
	I rule.	I shall rule.	I was ruling.
Sing. 1.	Reg-o	Reg-am	Reg-ēbam
2.	Reg-is	Reg-ēs	Reg-ēbās
3.	Reg-it	Reg-et	Reg-ēbat
Plur. 1.	Reg-imus	Reg-ēmus	Reg-ēbāmus
2.	Reg-itis	Reg-ētis	Reg-ēbātis
3.	Reg-unt	Reg-ent	Reg-ēbant.

PERFECT STEM, REX-.

Perfect.	*Future Perfect.*	*Pluperfect.*
I have ruled *or* I ruled	I shall have ruled.	I had ruled.
Sing. 1. Rex-i	Rex-ero	Rex-eram
2. Rex-isti	Rex-eris	Rex-erās
3. Rex-it	Rex-erit	Rex-erat
Plur. 1. Rex-imus	Rex-erimus	Rex-erāmus
2. Rex-istis	Rex-eritis	Rex-erātis
3. Rex-ērunt	Rex-erint	Rex-erant.

IMPERATIVE MOOD.

Present Tense.

Sing. 2. Reg-e, 'Rule thou.'   Plur. 2. Reg-ite, 'Rule ye.'

FOURTH CONJUGATION.

INDICATIVE MOOD.

AUDĪ-RE, 'TO HEAR.' PRESENT STEM, AUDĪ-.

Present.	*Future Simple.*	*Imperfect.*
I hear.	I shall hear.	I was hearing.
Sing. 1. Aud-io	Aud-iam	Aud-iēbam
2. Aud-īs	Aud-iēs	Aud-iēbās
3. Aud-it	Aud-iet	Aud-iēbat
Plur. 1. Aud-īmus	Aud-iēmus	Aud-iēbāmus
2. Aud-ītis	Aud-iētis	Aud-iēbātis
3. Aud-iunt	Aud-ient	Aud-iēbant.

PERFECT STEM, AUDĪV-.

Perfect.	*Future Perfect.*	*Pluperfect.*
I have heard *or* I heard.	I shall have heard.	I had heard.
Sing. 1. Audīv-i	Audīv-ero	Audīv-eram
2. Audīv-isti	Audīv-eris	Audīv-erās
3. Audīv-it	Audīv-erit	Audīv-erat
Plur. 1. Audīv-imus	Audīv-erimus	Audīv-erāmus
2. Audīv-istis	Audīv-eritis	Audīv-erātis
3. Audīv-ērunt	Audīv-erint	Audīv-erant.

IMPERATIVE MOOD.

Present Tense.

Sing. 2. Audī, 'Hear thou.'   Plur. 2. Audī-te, 'Hear ye.'

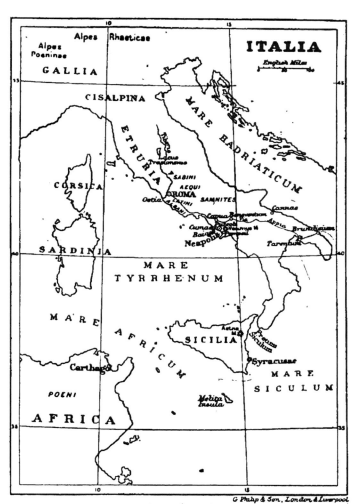

ITALIA

G. Philip & Son., London & Liverpool

GIVING A SOP TO CERBERUS. (From the Vatican Vergil.)

LATIN COURSE

EXERCISE I

NUMERALS.

CARDINAL.

1. Unus deus mundum creavit et gubernat.
2. Homini uni oculi duo, aures duae, bracchia duo sunt.
3. Tu caput unum habes, sed Cerberus, saevus Tartari custos, capita tria et tres linguas habebat.
4. Tres erant Gratiae vel deae pulchritudinis et formae.
5. Forma et pulchritudo trium Gratiarum omnibus Graecis notae erant.
6. Unius anni quattuor sunt tempora, ver, aestas, auctumnus, hiems.
7. Olympias erat spatium quattuor annorum, Graeci enim ludos Olympios post spatium quattuor annorum celebrabant.
8. Omne animal quinque corporis sensus habet.
9. Ex septem diebus sex sunt dies operarii.
10. Graeci praeclaros viros septem sapientes nominaverunt.

ASSAULT ON A TOWN.   (From a bas-relief on the walls of a Lycian tomb.)

EXERCISE II

1. Ex septem sapientibus Graecis maxime praeclari sunt Bias, Solon, Thales.
2. Septem erant mira aedificia vel miracula mundi.
3. Septem erant reges, septem montes Romae.
4. Novem erant Musae vel deae Carminum et Artium.
5. Novem erant libri Sibyllini, sed femina vetula sex ex novem libris cremavit.
6. Romani initio annum unum in decem modo menses dividebant.
7. Decem viri Romani leges Romanas quondam scribebant.
8. Decem viri agros publicos in cives dividebant.
9. Graeci milites annos decem Troiam oppugnabant.
10. Hercules duodecim opera finivit.

NUMERALS CARDINAL.

1. ūnus, -a, -um.
2. duo, -ae, -o.
3. trēs, tria.
4. quattuor.
5. quinque.
6. sex.
7. septem.
8. octō.
9. novem.
10. decem.
11. undecim.
12. duodecim.

A SIBYL. (From the Vatican Vergil.)

	M.	*F.*	*N.*
N.	du-o	du-ae	du-o
A.	du-ōs *or* du-o	du-ās	du-o
G.	du-ōrum	du-ārum	du-ōrum
D. and A.	du-ōbus	du-ābus	du-ōbus.

	M. F.	*N.*
N. A.	trēs	tria
G.	tri-um	tri-um
D. A.	tri-bus	tri-bus.

The **first three numerals** are declined; the others are indeclinable.

Unus is declined like *bonus*, except in the genitive and dative singular. The genitive singular is *ūnĭus* and dative singular *ūnĭ* for all genders.

After a numeral 'of' is generally translated before another numeral by *e* or *ex*, as *unus ex septem*, 'one of seven.'

EXERCISE III

ORDINAL NUMERALS.

Seven Kings of Rome, B.C. 753-509.

1. Romulus, primus rex Romanorum, urbem Romam designavit.
2. Numa Pompilius, secundus rex, Iani templum aedificavit.

3. Tullus Hostilius, tertius rex, Albanos et Sabinos superavit.

4. Ancus Marcius, quartus rex, Latinos socios in urbem Romam vocavit.

5. Tarquinius Priscus, quintus rex, in urbem Romam ex Etruriā migravit.

6. Quinti regis opera, in bello et in pace, magna fuerunt.

7. Servius Tullius, sextus rex, urbem muro cinxit.

8. Tarquinius Superbus erat septimus et ultimus rex.

9. Primo reges, secundo consules, tertio imperatores Romam regebant.

10. Tertia imperii species Romae perniciosa fuit.

1st prīmus.	7th septimus.	
2nd secundus.	8th octāvus.	ADVERBS.
3rd tertius.	9th nōnus.	
4th quartus.	10th decimus.	prīmō, firstly.
5th quintus.	11th undecimus.	secundō, secondly.
6th sextus.	12th duodecimus.	tertiō, thirdly.

Months of the Year.

Ianuārius—Februārius—Martius—Aprīlis — Maius — Iūnius Quintīlis *or* Iūlius—Sextīlis *or* Augustus—September—October—November—December.

The ordinals are declined like *bonus.*

The names of the months are really adjectives agreeing with *mensis* understood.

EXERCISE IV

Seven Wonders of the World.

1. Graeci antiqui septem ingentia monumenta orbis miracula appellabant.

2. Primo reges Aegyptii tria magna sepulcra in ripis Nili designaverunt.

3. Centum milia servorum unum et viginti annos monumenta ingentia aedificabant.

THE TOMB OF MAUSOLUS. (From a restoration in the British Museum.)

4. Primum sepulcrum quingentos pedes altum et octingentos pedes latum erat.

5. Secundum miraculum erat sepulcrum Mausoli, regis Cariae.

6. Artemisia, Mausoli uxor et regina, monumentum ingens marito suo struxit.

7. Sepulcrum autem centum quadraginta quinque pedes altum erat.

8. In summo monumento unae quadrigae quinquaginta duo pedes altae stabant.

9. Templum Dianae Ephesiae tertium locum in numero miraculorum habebat.

CARDINALS.

20	vīgintī	200	ducent-i, -ae, -a
30	trīginta	300	trecent-i, -ae, -a
40	quādraginta	400	quadringent-i, -ae, -a
50	quinquāginta	500	quingent-i, -ae, -a
60	sexāginta	600	sexcent-i, -ae, -a
70	septuāginta	700	septingent-i, -ae, -a
80	octōginta	800	octingent-i, -ae, -a
90	nonāginta	900	nongent-i, -ae, -a
100	centum	1000	mille

In compound numbers between twenty and one hundred the smaller with et comes first or the larger without et, as *duo et viginti* or *viginti duo*. Above a hundred the larger comes first, with or without et, as **centum et unus** or **centum viginti**.

Mille, in the singular, is an indeclinable adjective; as *mille milites*, 'a thousand soldiers.'

Mille, in the plural, is declined as a neuter substantive; N. and A. *mīl*-ia, G. *mīl*-ium, D. and A. *mīl*-ibus. *Duo milia militum*, 'two thousand soldiers.' But if other numerals come between, it is not followed by a genitive, as *duo milia ducenti milites*, 'two thousand two hundred soldiers.'

Accusative of Space. In answer to the questions 'how high?' 'how long?' 'how broad?' 'how deep?' 'how far?' the Accusative is used. Murus ducentos pedes altus, '*a wall two hundred feet high.*'

EXERCISE V

1. Semiramis, Babylonia regina, quartum miraculum aedificavit.
2. Ex columnis, ducentos pedes altis, hortus ingens pendebat.
3. In urbe Babylone centum aeneae portae et ducentae quinquaginta turres in moenibus erant.
4. Ingens Apollinis figura locum quintum habebat.

5. Aenea statua centum viginti unum pedes alta erat et inter pedes magnae figurae naves navigabant.
6. Signum Iovis Olympii sextum locum in numero miraculorum habet.
7. Iovis signum, praeclarum Phidiae opus, templum Olympium ornabat.
8. Septimum et ultimum miraculum erat Pharus Alexandrina.
9. Pharus, turris alta in insulā, nomen ab insulā habebat.
10. Ex septem miraculis sepulcra regum Aegyptiorum hodie supersunt.

A LIGHTHOUSE. (From a bas-relief in the Torlonia Museum, Rome.)

PRACTISING JUMPING IN THE GYMNASIUM. (From a painting on a drinking-cup, &c.)

EXERCISE VI

INFINITIVE MOOD.	PRESENT TENSE.
First Conjugation.	Amā-re, 'to love.'
Second Conjugation.	Monē-re, 'to advise.'
Third Conjugation.	Reg-e-re, 'to rule.'
Fourth Conjugation.	Audī-re, 'to hear.'

Dialogue on the Choice of a Game.

Puer 1. Tempus est ludere. De genere lusus iam consultare possumus.

Puer 2. Ego vestras sententias audire opto.

Puer 3. Ego pilā ludere studeo. Ita enim omnes corporis partes exercere poterimus.

Puer 4. Iucundum est certare cursu. Difficile est omnibus placere.

Puer 5. Omnes contendere saltu possumus, sed mediā aestate currere non potestis.

Puer 6. Non possumus te audire. Tu si consilio vincere non potueris, fraude superare poteris.

Puer 1. Sententiam tuam rogare necesse non est. Semper monere, nunquam parere, potes.

Pueri multi. Nos omnes cursu certare optamus. Necesse erit properare aut certamen finire non poterimus.

Puer 2. Cursu certare paene omnes studemus. Necesse t stadium designare.

The verb **possum**, which is compounded of the root *pot-* (able) and *sum*, is somewhat irregular.

Present Tense. *Pos*-sum, *pot*-es, *pot*-est ; *pos*-sumus, *pot*-estis, *pos*-sunt.

Future Simple, *pot*-ero ; imperfect, *pot*-eram ; perfect, *pot*-ui ; future-perfect, *pot*-uero ; pluperfect, *pot*-ueram.

EXERCISE VII

INFINITIVE MOOD. PRESENT TENSE.

LAUREL CROWN.

Dialogue (continued).

Puer 1. Properare necesse est, si lusum ante tenebras finire studemus.

Puer 2. Necesse est praemia victori dare.

Puer 3. Nonne sine praemiis contendere poteritis ?

Puer 4. Stulti est pro pecuniā certare.

Puer 5. Sapientis est pro gloriā modo contendere.

Puer 6. Satis erit victorem coronā, honoris causā, ornare.

Puer 7. Ego virtute, non fraude, superare studeo.

Puer 1. Humanum est errare. Stulti est ante proelium gaudere.

Puer 2. Virtutem habere non satis est, sed exercere necesse est.

Puer 3. Necesse erit a me victoriam reportare.

Puer 4. Facile est te arte superare.

Puer 5. Tempus est ad urbem properare. Necesse erit cras certamen finire.

Magister 1. Puerorum est tempus contentione consumere.

Magister 2. Facile est pueros monere, difficile regere.

A **genitive** is sometimes used with the verb 'to be,' and followed by an Infinitive, where in English it is necessary to supply a word like 'nature,' 'mark,' 'part,' &c.

Puerorum est ludere. *It is the nature of boys to play.*

ROMAN GARDEN. (From Pompeian wall-paintings.)

EXERCISE VIII
COMPARISON OF ADJECTIVES.

POSITIVE.	COMPARATIVE.	SUPERLATIVE.
Trist-is, 'sad.'	Trist-ior, 'sadder,' or 'more sad.'	Trist-issimus, 'saddest,' or 'most sad.'

	Singular.		*Plural.*	
	M. and F.	*N.*	*M. and F.*	*N.*
Nom.	Tristior	Tristius	Tristior-es	Tristior-a
Acc.	Tristior-em	Tristius	Tristior-es	Tristior-a
Gen.	Tristior-is		Tristior-um	
Dat.	Tristior-i		Tristior-ibus	
Abl.	Tristior-e		Tristior-ibus	

On Friendship.

1. Nihil dulcius est in vitā quam amicitia firmissima.
2. Et secundas res splendidiores reddit amicitia con-
    iunctissima et adversas leviores.
3. Res adversae sine amicis oneri gravissimo sunt.
4. Nihil praestantius, nihil firmius est quam cum viris
    honestissimis amicitia.
5. Nihil est amabilius aut praestantius virtute : vitam
    enim tutiorem et opulentiorem reddit.

6. Vitam sine amicis semper gravissimam et tristissimam puto.
7. Patriae iura sola sunt sanctiora quam amicitiae.
8. Rarissimae, sed praeclarissimae sunt, coniunctissimae amicitiae.
9. Stultissimum est amicos, iucundissima vitae ornamenta, non parare.
10. Cicero, scriptor praeclarissimus, nihil amicitiā praestantius aut utilius putavit.

The Comparative is formed by adding -ior and the **Superlative** by adding -issimus to the last consonant of the stem of the Positive; as positive, long-us; comparative, long-ior; superlative, long-issimus.

Comparison. If two substantives are compared by means of a comparative and the conjunction **quam**, 'than,' both substantives are in the same case.

Dies longiores quam noctes sunt.
The days are longer than the nights.

Ablative of Comparison. The thing compared may be put in the Ablative Case when the Nom. or Acc. would have been used with **quam**.

Dies longiores sunt noctibus. *The days are longer than the nights.*

EXERCISE IX

IMPERATIVE MOOD. PRESENT TENSE.
The Verb SUM, 'I am.'

Es, 'be thou.'   Este, 'be ye.'

First Conjug.   Am-ā, 'love thou.'   Am-āte, 'love ye.'
Second Conjug. Mon-ē, 'advise thou.'   Mon-ēte, 'advise ye.'
Third Conjug.   Reg-e, 'rule thou.'   Reg-ite, 'rule ye.'
Fourth Conjug. Aud-ī, 'hear thou.'   Aud-īte, 'hear ye.'

A few verbs of the third conjugation drop the final -e in the second person singular of the present imperative. The most common are dīc, 'say thou,' dīc-ite, 'say ye'; dūc, 'lead thou,' dūc-ite, 'lead ye'; fac, 'make thou,' fac-ite, 'make ye.'

ROMAN MODE OF RECLINING AT DINNER. (From a bas-relief.)

Dialogue. A Banquet.

ANTE CENAM.

m Echīni, 'sea-urchins.' Asparagi, 'asparagus.'
f Ostreae, 'oysters.' Balani, 'mussels.'
m Turdi, 'thrushes.' Gallina altilis, 'a large fowl.'

IN CENĀ.

Sinciput aprugnum, 'boar's- Lepores, 'hares.'
  head.' Muraenae, 'salt-water eels.
Anates, 'ducks.' Panes Picentes, 'bread from
Mulli, 'mullets.'   Picenum.'

SECUNDA MENSA.

Pira, 'pears.' Olīvae, 'olives.'
Pōma, 'apples.' Castaneae, 'chestnuts.

Hospes 1. Huc ades, puer! Monstra viam ad Caesaris hortos!

Puer. Hinc flectite ad dextram, tum cursum ad sinistram dirigite!

Hospes 1. Properate, comites! Este bono animo!

Hospes 2. Manete, paulisper! Cavete! E via erramus!

Hospes 3. Tace, stulte! Ecce ostium! Pulsate!

Magister. Salvete, amici ! Date puero in manum tegumenta vestra !

Hospes 1. Salve, optime amice ! Da veniam, si sero adsumus.

Magister. Ad tempus adestis. Puer, duc nos ad triclinium !

Hospes 2. Es tu prior, si libet !

Magister. Removete moram ! Heus, adeste huc !

Hospes 3. Spectate tabulas ! Quam pulchrum est atrium !

Magister. Heus, puer, ministra aquam !

Hospes 1. Lava tu prior !

Hospes 2. Sta rectus, puer ! Da mihi linteum !

Magister. Lavate et accumbite ! Designate lectos ! Ego in summo lecto accumbam. Tu prope me lectum delige ! Tu infra accumbe !

Hospes 3. Move te, si libet ! Non est locus mihi.

Hospes 4. Da veniam ! Accumbe prior !

Magister. Heus, pueri, ministrate cenam ! Demite soleas ! Praebete vos hilares, amici.

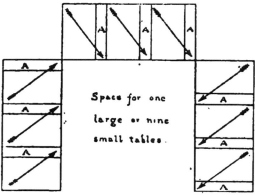

PLAN OF A TRICLINIUM SEATED FOR NINE. (The arrows indicate the position of the diners and A the cushions.)

In all four conjugations the present imperative singular can be formed from the **present infinitive** by taking away the final syllable -re. In each case the imperative is the same as the present stem except in the third conjugation, where the final -e of the imperative does not appear in the present stem.

EXERCISE X

IMPERATIVE MOOD. PRESENT TENSE.

DRINKING-CUP.
(British Museum.)

Dialogue at a Banquet (continued).

Hospes 1. Narra, si libet, fabulam tuam!

Hospes 2. Mane promisso tuo!

Magister. Serva fabulas et recita apud secundam mensam! Funde vinum et bibe!

Hospes 3. Mihi aquam modo da!

Magister. Date panem, pueri! Satis est ostrearum! Apponite anates! Discerpite gallinam!

Hospes 4. Tibi serva muraenam! Scinde mihi alam gallinae!

Hospes 1. Ecce poculum pulchrum! Lege titulum, si libet!

Hospes 2 (*legit*). 'Me vino imple! Misce, amice! Tum bibe et reple!'

Hospes 3. Funde mihi aquam ad dimidium poculum! Tum vino imple more antiquo!

Magister. Properate, pueri! Quam tardi estis! Tollite muraenam et anates! Tum date secundam mensam!

Hospes 1. Ecce poma! Da, puer, olivas!

Hospes 2. Iam satis. Remove fructus! Age nunc magistro gratias!

Hospes 3. Age tu prior!

Magister. Surgite, amici, a mensā! Portate, pueri, soleas! Iam ludite vel cantate, amici, si libet!

EXERCISE XI

IRREGULAR COMPARISON OF ADJECTIVES.

POSITIVE.	COMPARATIVE.	SUPERLATIVE.
Bonus, 'good.'	Melior, 'better.'	Optimus, 'best.'
Magnus, 'great.'	Maior, 'greater.'	Maximus, 'greatest.'
Malus, 'bad.'	Peior, 'worse.'	Pessimus, 'worst.'
Multus, 'much.'	Plus, 'more' (neut.)	Plurimus, 'most.'
Parvus, 'small.'	Minor, 'less' (smaller).	Minimus, 'least.'

Adjectives ending in -er form the superlative by adding -rimus, as celer, celer-ior, celer-rimus; niger, nigr-ior, niger-rimus (adjectives like niger drop the e in the comparative).

Six adjectives in -lis form the superlative by adding -limus to the stem: as facil-is, 'easy,' facil-ior, facil-limus.

Also difficilis, *difficult*; similis, *like*; dissimilis, *unlike*; gracilis, *slender*; humilis, *humble*.

Plūs (*gen.* plūris, *dat. and abl.* plūri) in singular is only used in neuter. Plural, nom. and acc. plūres, neut. plūra, gen. plūrium, dat. and abl. plūribus.

Alexander the Great.

1. Nunquam vir maior aut melior Alexandro, rege Macedonum, fuit.
2. Romani antiqui Iovem Optimum Maximum appellabant.
3. Macedones quoque Alexandrum virum optimum et maximum putabant.
4. Plurimas et maximas in Asiā civitates superavit Alexander; quo plures superavit, eo plures oppugnavit.

ADVERBS.

The positive adverb usually ends in -ē, but those formed from adjectives of the third declension often end in -ter, and a few are irregular.

The comparative adverb ends in -us, and is the same as the neuter of the comparative adjective. The superlative adverb ends in -ē. Thus—

ANCIENT BABYLON.

POSITIVE.	COMPARATIVE.	SUPERLATIVE.
Longē, 'far.'	Longius.	Longissimē.
Bene, 'well.'	Melius.	Optimē.
Fortiter, 'bravely.'	Fortius.	Fortissimē.
Magnopere, 'greatly.'	Magis.	Maximē.

GENERAL ADDRESSING HIS
ARMY.

EXERCISE XII

PASSIVE VOICE.

FIRST CONJUGATION.

INDICATIVE MOOD.

PRESENT TENSE.	FUTURE SIMPLE.
I am loved *or* I am being loved.	I shall be loved.

		PRESENT	FUTURE
Sing.	1.	Am-or	Am-ābor
	2.	Am-āris	Am-āberis
	3.	Am-ātur	Am-ābitur
Plur.	1.	Am-āmur	Am-ābimur
	2.	Am-āmini	Am-ābimini
	3.	Am-antur	Am-ābuntur.

A General exhorts his Troops.

1. Postero die militum concilium a duce convocatur.
2. Milites fessi verbis multis et acribus ad proelium incitantur.
3. 'Milites, incommodo nostro nimis perturbamini.'
4. 'Neque virtute neque in acie nos a Romanis superamur.'
5. 'Cur vos, viri fortes et strenui, adeo metu sollicitamini?'
6. 'Non sic victoria a vobis reportabitur: non sic hostium arces expugnabuntur.'
7. 'Ego tamen propter vestram ignaviam maximis doloribus crucior.'
8. 'Victoria mox reportabitur, si fortuna mutabitur.'
9. 'In bello proelia secunda a me non semper exspectantur.'

10. 'Si vulnerabimini aut superabimini, vos in magno honore cives semper habebunt.'

11. 'Si tamen mors honesta turpi fugā vitabitur, a fortibus semper culpabimur et vituperabimur.'

12. 'Virtus igitur et fortitudo iam postulantur et exspectabuntur.'

The Agent. After a passive verb, the agent or person by whom the action is performed is put in the ablative case with the preposition **ā** *or* **ab**, the **Subject** of the **Active** verb becoming the **Agent** after the **Passive** verb.

Active.	Passive.
Dux concilium convocat.	Concilium a duce convocatur.
The general calls a council.	*A council is called by the general.*

Note. The preposition **ā** or **ab** must only be used with the name of a person, and must not precede the **ablative** of the **instrument**.

Dux hastā vulneratur.
The general is wounded by a spear.

EXERCISE XIII

INDICATIVE MOOD. IMPERFECT TENSE.

I was being loved *or* I was loved, *or* I used to be loved.

Sing.	1. Am-ābar	*Plur.*	1. Am-ābāmur
	2. Am-ābāris		2. Am-ābāmini
	3. Am-ābātur		3. Am-ābantur.

Frugality in Ancient Rome.

1. Apud Romanos antiquos integritas vitae laudabatur et frugalitas pluris quam argentum aestimabatur.

2. Paupertas magni, divitiae parvi aestimabantur.

3. Luxuria privata a bonis civibus damnabatur; simplicitas praedicabatur.

4. Virtus et fortitudo et sapientia postulabantur et amabantur.

5. Si bonis exemplis incitabimur, multa vitia a nobis vitabuntur.
6. Exempla bona Romanorum paulisper a nobis explorabuntur et spectabuntur.
7. Optimae morum regulae servabantur et amabantur.
8. Vita rustica et humilis laudabatur: vita luxuriosa culpabatur et repudiabatur.
9. Non pecunia sed potestas a civibus optabatur.
10. Multa et praeclara exempla nobis ab honestis viris mandabantur.

EXERCISE XIV
DEMONSTRATIVE PRONOUN.

Is, 'THAT'; 'HE,' 'SHE,' 'IT.'

| | *Singular.* | | | *Plural.* | | |
	M.	*F.*	*N.*	*M.*	*F.*	*N.*
Nom.	Is	ea	id	Eī *or* iī	eae	ea
Acc.	Eum	eam	id	Eōs	eās	ea
Gen.	Eius	ēius	ēius	Eōrum	eārum	eōrum
Dat.	Eī	eī	eī	Eīs *or* iīs	Eīs *or* iīs	Eīs *or* iīs
Abl.	Eō	eā	eō	Eīs *or* iīs	Eīs *or* iīs	Eīs *or* iīs.

Alexander in Asia.

1. Ubi ea res nuntiata est, Alexander milites suos convocavit.
2. Multae res eum ad pugnam incitabant.
3. Itaque signum pugnae ab eo statim datur.
4. Sed ea pugna regi et comitibus eius paene exitio erat.
5. Contra eum Dareus fortissimos e militibus suis instruxerat.
6. Subito in eius currum Persae impetum suum dabant.
7. Nec defuit ei perpetua in dubiis rebus felicitas.

8. Amici eius ad auxilium undique properant.

9. Tandem rex id periculum feliciter vitavit.

10. Post eas res milites suos in urbem Babylonem duxit.

BATTLE-SCENE BETWEEN GREEKS AND PERSIANS.
(From the Pompeian mosaic of the battle of Issus.)

Hitherto the possessive pronouns **his, her, its, their** have **always been reflexive**, that is, have referred to the subject of the sentence, and have been translated by the **reflexive pronoun suus**.

But if these pronouns **his, her, its, their** do not refer to the subject but to some other substantive, they must be translated by the genitives of the pronoun **is**, that is by **eius** in the singular and **eorum** in the plural.

Alexander milites **suos** incitat.
Alexander urges on his (Alexander's) soldiers.

Alexander bellum Persis indicit et **eorum** agros vastat.
Alexander declares war on the Persians and lays waste their (the Persians') fields.

EXERCISE XV

	PERFECT.	FUTURE PERFECT.	PLUPERFECT.
	I have been *or* was loved.	I shall have been loved.	I had been loved.
Sing. 1.	Amātus sum	Amātus ero	Amātus eram
2.	Amātus es	Amātus eris	Amātus erās
3.	Amātus est	Amātus erit	Amātus erat
Plur. 1.	Amāti sumus	Amāti erimus	Amāti erāmus
2.	Amāti estis	Amāti eritis	Amāti erātis
3.	Amāti sunt	Amāti erunt	Amāti erant.

In the passive voice the perfect tenses are formed from the perfect participle **amātus** and the present tenses of the verb **sum.**

The perfect participle **amātus** must always agree in gender and number with the subject.

The **principal parts** of a verb are the 1st person of the present tense, the present infinitive, the 1st person of the perfect tense, and the supine in -um. From these **parts all** the tenses of a verb can be formed.[A] The perfect participle is formed by changing the final -m of the supine into -s, as **amātum, amātus.**

Hence the principal parts of the four conjugations may be shown thus :

PRESENT.	INFINITIVE.	PERFECT.	SUPINE.
Am-o	Am-āre	Amāv-i	Amā-tum
Mon-eo	Mon-ēre	Monu-i	Moni-tum
Reg-o	Reg-ere	Rex-i	Rec-tum
Aud-io	Aud-īre	Audīv-i	Audī-tum.

Frugality at Rome.

CINCINNATUS, CURIUS, AND FABRICIUS.

1. Praeclarum exemplum a Cincinnato memoriae mandatum est.

2. Roma olim ab Aequis oppugnata erat; milites Romani superabantur; agri vastabantur.

3. Tum Cincinnatus, agricola humilis, ab aratro ad dictaturam vocatus est.

4. Consuli Romano auxilium ab eo datum est; Roma
   timore liberata est; hostes superati et fugati
   sunt.

5. Tum omnia praemia a Cincinnato repudiata sunt;
   omnis praeda militibus data est.

6. Curius et Fabricius non minus laudabuntur, si
   eorum exempla diligenter considerata erunt.

PLOUGHING. (From a bas-relief.)

7. Ei enim a Samnitibus pecuniā tentati et sollicitati
   erant: ab eis munera repudiata sunt.

8. Luxuria a Fabricio culpata et vituperata est;
   frugalitas laudata et praedicata est.

9. Pecunia a Curio minimi aestimata est; imperium
   amatum et optatum est.

10. Si praeclara exempla eorum civium a nobis servata
    erunt, fortuna nostra non mutabitur.

EXERCISE XVI

PARTITIVE GENITIVE

AFTER ADVERBS AND NEUTER ADJECTIVES.

Decline of Roman morals.

1. Romanis antiquis non minus animi quam fidei erat.
2. Id enim temporis duces multum auctoritatis apud cives habebant.
3. Praeclarum Curi responsum parum eloquentiae, satis sapientiae habet.
4. 'Non ego plus pecuniae sed plus auctoritatis habere opto.'
5. Id exemplum gravitatis et ponderis plurimum habet.
6. Sed post bellum Punicum minimum gravitatis minimumque honestatis apud Romanos erat.
7. Unde plurimum periculi Latino generi erat.
8. Nihil potestatis penes populum, nimis penes senatum erat.
9. Sapientia minus auctoritatis quam pecunia habebat.
10. Itaque Romani in multis bellis civilibus satis poenarum dabant.

A **genitive** is often used after adverbs or neuter adjectives of quantity, such as *multum, plus, plurimum, parum, minus, minimum, nihil, satis, nimis,* &c. ; as **multum pecuniae,** 'much money' ; **nihil honestatis,** 'no honour.'

EXERCISE XVII

ACTIVE AND PASSIVE TENSES.

Dialogue between the Ghosts of Xerxes and Leonidas.

[Xerxes, king of Persia, B.C. 485-465, invaded Greece with an enormous army in B.C. 480. Leonidas, the king of Sparta, and 300 of his subjects perished in defending the Pass of Thermopylae against the Persians.]

Xerxes. Amplissimis honoribus et praemiis, Leonida, a me decoratus es!

Leonidas. Neque gloriam neque honores, Rex Magne, ego optavi.

Xerxes. Tu autem, honoris causā, minister et satelles Regis Magni nominatus es!

Leonidas. Eheu! Frustra te vitare studui. Valde ego delectatus eram quod tu apud mortuos vitatus eras.

Xerxes. Quid! Nonne ego ab omnibus hominibus honoribus cumulatus sum? Num a te, trecentorum latronum duce, probris vexabor et onerabor?

Leonidas. Nos trecenti a barbaris tuis necati neque superati sumus! Numero, non virtute, debellatus sum.

Xerxes. Quid! Num copiae tuae cum meis comparabuntur?

Leonidas. Triginta milia Persarum a trecentis morti data sunt. Nonne Manes militum tuorum hic in ripā spectas?

Xerxes. Res stulta a te tentata est.

Leonidas. Valde errasti! Vos exemplo nostro exanimati et defatigati estis, Graeci autem ad maiorem spem incitati sunt.

Xerxes. Attica a me vastata erat. Dolore crucior quod agri tui non vexati sunt.

Leonidas. Neque iniuriis tuis olim incitatus sum, neque laudibus tuis nunc incitor. Non iam Rex Magnus appellaberis. Ecce! Minos, iudex severus, te vocat. Vale!

The interrogative particle **num** always expects a negative answer, while **nonne** expects a positive answer.

Nonne amicum amas?	**Amo.**
Do you not love your friend?	*I do.*
Num inimicum amas?	**Non amo.**
You do not love an enemy, do you?	*I do not.*

EXERCISE XVIII

DEMONSTRATIVE PRONOUNS. HĬC AND ILLE.

Hĭc, 'THIS' (near me); *or* 'HE,' 'SHE,' 'IT'; 'THE LATTER.'

	Singular.			*Plural.*		
	M.	*F.*	*N.*	*M.*	*F.*	*N.*
Nom.	Hĭc	haec	hŏc	Hī	hae	haec
Acc.	Hunc	hanc	hŏc	Hōs	hās	haec
Gen.	Hūius	hūius	hūius	Hōrum	hārum	hōrum
Dat.	Huĭc	huĭc	huĭc	Hīs	hīs	hīs
Abl.	Hŏc	hāc	hŏc	Hīs	hīs	hīs.

Ille, 'THAT' (yonder); *or* 'HE,' 'SHE,' 'IT'; 'THE FORMER.'

	M.	*F.*	*N.*	*M.*	*F.*	*N.*
Nom.	Ille	illa	illud	Illī	illae	illa
Acc.	Illum	illam	illud	Illōs	illās	illa
Gen.	Illĭus	illĭus	illĭus	Illōrum	illārum	illōrum
Dat.	Illī	illī	illī	Illīs	illīs	illīs
Abl.	Illŏ	illā	illŏ	Illīs	illīs	illīs.

Iste. 'THAT' (near you) is declined like Ille.

The Stoics and Epicureans.

1. Cicero, orator ille Romanus, haec verba olim dixit:
2. 'Ex illis philosophis multi huic civitati saluti fuerunt.'
3. Inter illos philosophos praeclari erant Zeno et Epicurus, sed hic ab illo longe diversus.
4. Huius scholae discipuli Epicurei, illius Stoici nominantur.
5. Epicurei felicitatem huius vitae voluptate terminant.
6. Ab hac diversa fuit illorum sententia; illi enim maximum vitae bonum in honestate, hi in vita beata ponunt.

7. Magno illi Diogeni dissimillimus erat Epicurus.
8. Illi enim frugalitas, huic luxuria curae erat.
9. Cynicus autem ille illam luxuriam non virtutem sed animi mollitiam putavit.

DIOGENES AND ALEXANDER THE GREAT. (From sculpture.)

10. Digna sunt memoriā ista verba illius Cynici 'Nunc paululum a sole.'
11. Istis enim verbis Diogenes unam suam voluntatem Alexandro significavit.

The pronouns **hic** and **ille** may be used like adjectives in agreement with substantives or alone as demonstrative pronouns. **Hic** means 'the latter' or 'the nearer,' and **ille**, 'the former' or 'the more distant' if they are used in contrast.

Ille when used with a proper name, or a substantive in apposition to a proper name, often means the 'famous.'

Cicero, orator ille.   Magnus ille Alexander.
Cicero, the famous orator. *The Great Alexander.*

EXERCISE XIX

PASSIVE VOICE. SECOND CONJUGATION.

INDICATIVE MOOD.

		PRESENT TENSE.	FUTURE SIMPLE.	IMPERFECT.
		I am advised *or* I am being advised.	I shall be advised.	I was being advised.
Sing.	1.	Mone-or	Monĕ-bor	Monĕ-bar
	2.	Monĕ-ris	Monĕ-beris	Monĕ-bāris
	3.	Monĕ-tur	Monĕ-bitur	Monĕ-bātur
Plur.	1.	Monĕ-mur	Monĕ-bimur	Monĕ-bāmur
	2.	Monĕ-mini	Monĕ-bimini	Monĕ-bāmini
	3.	Mone-ntur	Monĕ-buntur	Monĕ-bantur.

Dialogue between the Ghosts of Achilles and Homer.

Achilles. Gaudio compleor, praeclarissime poeta, quod fama tua mihi debetur.

Homer. Nempe fabula satis digna a te praebebatur. Ulixi autem magis quam tibi gratia debetur et habebitur.

Achilles. Quid! Fama tua magis dolo quam virtute augetur! Gratia omnis Ulixi habetur! Num ego a societate laudis prohibebor?

Homer. Irā tuā non ego terrebor. Vano furore compleris. Nonne exemplo horum Manium moneberis et doceberis?

Achilles. Decem annos Troia obsidebatur. Ego a Troianis maxime timebar. Fama carminis tui factis meis debetur.

Homer. Verbis tuis moveor, praeclare miles, sed sententiā tuā non deterrebor.

Achilles. Eheu! Mors mea defletur! Memoria deletur!

Homer. Naturā docemur et monemur! Memoria factorum tuorum mox delebitur nisi carminibus meis augebitur et ornabitur.

Achilles. Verba tua memoriā tenebuntur, sed de sententiā meā non deterrebor.

DEATH OF ACHILLES.   (From a bas-relief.)

EXERCISE XX

INTERROGATIVE PRONOUN.

QUIS, 'WHO?'   QUID, 'WHAT?'

	Sing.			*Plur.*		
	M.	**F.**	**N.**	**M.**	**F.**	**N.**
Nom.	Quis	quis	quid	Qui	quae	quae
	Qui	quae	quod			
Acc.	Quem	quam	quid *or* quod	Quōs	quās	quae
Gen.	Cūius	cūius	cūius	Quōrum	quārum	quōrum
Dat.	Cuī	cuī	cuī	Quibus	Quibus	quibus
Abl.	Quō	quā	quō	Quibus	Quibus	quibus.

The forms **quis** and **quid** are used as strict interrogative pronouns, while **qui, quae, quod** are used as interrogative adjectives agreeing with a substantive.

Quis es? *Who art thou?*
Qui homo es? *What man art thou?*
Quid portas? *What dost thou bring?*
Quod donum portas? *What gift dost thou bring?*

Dialogue between Alexander the Great and a Scythian Chief.

Scythian. Quis es? Quā de causā (in) regnum nostrum intravisti?

Alexander. Quid dicis? Quo in oppido habitas? Qui homo in toto orbe terrarum Alexandrum ignorat?

Scythian. Quis autem est Alexander? Quid optas? Quam ob causam ades?

Alexander. Quae verba audio? Quā audaciā incitaris?

Scythian. E quibus regionibus exercitum duxisti?

Alexander. Quae litora ego non spectavi? Quis clarior Alexandro? Cui ego non notus sum?

Scythian. Si praedae causā in patriam nostram intravisti, quibus donis contentus eris? Quā praedā sitim tuam satiare poterimus?

Alexander. Quibus condicionibus amicitiam et foedus nobiscum iunges?

Scythian. Quo modo amicitia inter servum et dominum esse potest?

Alexander. Cui non ego leges aequas dedi? Cuius iniuriae memor es?

Scythian. Qui peior latro in toto orbe terrarum est?

Alexander. Quid pluribus verbis opus est? Bellum parate! Quorum auxilium iam postulabis?

Alinari photo.] ALEXANDER THE GREAT.
(From a bronze statue in the Naples Museum.)

Scythian. Quam ob rem nos tibi servire debemus? Fortes fortuna iuvat. Ad bellum parati sumus.

The preposition **cum**, 'with,' instead of preceding the pronouns, mē, tē, sē, nōbis, vōbis, and the Relative, follows and is joined to them, as mē-cum, 'with me,' nōbis-cum, 'with us,' **quibus-cum**, 'with whom,' &c.

BATTLEFIELD OF CANNAE.

EXERCISE XXI

·SECOND CONJUGATION.

PERFECT STEM.

PERFECT TENSE.	FUTURE PERFECT	PLUPERFECT.
Monitus sum.	Monitus ero.	Monitus eram.
I have been advised *or* I was advised.	I shall have been advised.	I had been advised.

Battle of Cannae. B.C. 216.

1. In pugnā Cannensi exercitus Romanus deletus erat
2. Tum Hannibal a duce forti sic monitus est.
3. 'Urbs minimo praesidio tenetur: cives metu territi sunt.'
4. 'Delectus undique habentur, sed adventus noster timetur.'

5. 'Si verbis meis doctus eris, urbs Roma mox delebitur.'

6. 'Cives fugā prohibebuntur, si urbs statim obsessa erit.'

7. 'Si exemplo meo doceberis, Roma delebitur, gloria tua augebitur.'

8. Hannibal sic monitus est, sed a bonis consiliis deterritus est.

9. Roma non est obsessa: urbs non est deleta.

10. Militum Romanorum virtus aucta est: multos post annos Carthago a Romanis deleta est.

EXERCISE XXII

RELATIVE PRONOUN.

QUI, 'WHO,' 'WHICH.'

Singular.

	M.	F.	N.	English. (Sing. and Plur.)
Nom.	Qui	quae	quod	Who
Acc.	Quem	quam	quod	Whom
Gen.	Cūius	cūius	cūius	Whose
Dat.	Cuī	cuī	cuī	To whom
Abl.	Quō	quā	quō	By whom.

Plural.

	M.	F.	N.	or
Nom.	Qui	quae	quae	Which
Acc.	Quōs	quās	quae	Which
Gen.	Quōrum	quārum	quōrum	Of which
Dat.	Quibus	quibus	quibus	To which
Abl.	Quibus	quibus	quibus	By which.

Story of Carthage.

First Punic War.   B.C. 264–241.

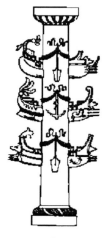

ROSTRAL COLUMN OF
C. DUILIUS.

1. Erat in Africā urbs Carthago, cuius incolae Poeni vocabantur.
2. Mox Poeni, quibus multae naves erant, in Siciliam navigabant.
3. Tum Romani, quorum in tutelā erant multa oppida in Siciliā, bellum cum Poenis commove-runt.
4. In Siciliā victoria penes Romanos stetit, quos tamen Poeni graviter vexabant.
5. Poeni enim rebus maritimis, quarum Romani imperiti fuerant, superiores erant.
6. Quinto autem anno Romani classem paraverunt, quā Poenos oppugnaverunt.
7. Magnam victoriam, quae Romanis gratissima fuit, reportavit consul Duilius.
8. Deinde Claudius, quem Romani consulem loco Duili creaverunt, ad Siciliam navigavit.
9. Verba stultissima, quibus Claudius consules priores culpavit, memoriae mandata sunt.
10. 'Illo die, quo hostium classem videbo, bello finem imponam.'
11. Dei, qui Romanis propitii fuerant, eum ob superbiam, quā irritati erant, crudeliter puniverunt.
12. Poeni enim, quos spes iam destituebat, magnam victoriam reportaverunt.

CARTHAGE.

Photochrom Co. Ltd. photo.]

AGREEMENT OF THE RELATIVE PRONOUN.

Agreement of Relative. The Relative agrees in Gender, Number and Person with its Antecedent (that is, the Substantive to which it refers), but its case depends on its position in its own clause.

. Case of the Relative. The Case depends on the place the Relative occupies in its own clause, which must not be confused with the principal sentence. If the Relative immediately precedes its own verb in English, it will generally be in the Nominative Case, because it is the Subject of the verb, but if a Substantive or Pronoun separates the Relative and its verb, it will generally be governed by the verb or by a preposition.

RELATIVE CLAUSE IN BRACKETS.

Nominative.   Vir (**qui** rebus suis contentus est) beatus est.
The man (who is contented with his own things) is happy.

Accusative.   Liber (**quem** habes) mihi est.
The book (which you have) is mine.

Genitive.   Vir (**cuius** exemplum laudas) adest.
The man (whose example you are praising) is present.

Dative.   Ille vir est (**cui** patriae salus dulcis est).
He is a man (to whom the safety of his country is sweet).

Ablative.   Urbs (**in quā** habito) Roma vocatur.
The city (in which I live) is called Rome.

ROMAN WAR-SHIPS. (From Pompeian wall-painting.)

EXERCISE XXIII

Story of Carthage (continued).

Second Punic War. B.C. 218–201.

1. Deinde Regulus, cui bellum mandatum erat, cum exercitu Romano in Africam navigavit.
2. Poeni autem, quibus Graeci auxilio erant, Romanos magna clade fugaverunt.
3. Pax, quam Poeni postulaverant, a Romanis est repudiata.
4. Tum Regulus, quem barbari omnibus suppliciis cruciaverant, crudeliter necatus est.
5. Pax, quam Poeni impetraverunt, duodeviginti annos servata est.
6. Erat autem in Hispania Saguntum oppidum cuius cives Poenorum potestatem timebant.
7. Mox Poeni, quorum dux Hannibal magnum exercitum comparaverat, hoc oppidum oppugnavit.
8. Quod ubi audiverunt Romani, bellum Poenis indixerunt.

9. Hannibal autem milites, quos in Hispaniā habebat, in Italiam per Alpes statim duxit.
10. Multis in proeliis, e quibus clades Cannensis Romanis gravissima fuit, Poeni victores fuerunt.

EXERCISE XXIV

Story of Carthage (continued).

Third Punic War. B.C. 146.

1. Anno belli quarto decimo Scipio, qui multa in Hispaniā bene gesserat, consul creatus est.
2. Is, cui Romani magnam fidem habebant, Poenorum exercitum profligavit.
3. Quā de clade ubi senatus Carthaginiensis audivit, Hannibal ex Italiā revocatus est.
4. Scipio autem, cuius exercitus equitibus maxime valebat, iterum exercitum hostium in Africā fugavit.
5. Poeni pacem, quam postulaverant, duris condicionibus impetraverunt.
6. Paucos post annos Romani, quorum duces adhuc Poenos timebant, tertium bellum commoverunt.
7. Deinde Carthago, quae tres-annos obsessa erat, expugnata est.
8. Aedificia et moenia, quae decori et praesidio urbi fuerant, deleta sunt.
9. Triumphum egit Scipio, cui etiam cognomen Africani datum est, quod eius avus antea habuerat.
10. Itaque Carthago, cuius potestate Romani territi erant, deleta et solo aequata est.

EXERCISE XXV

FIRST AND SECOND CONJUGATIONS.

PASSIVE INDICATIVE.

Dialogue between a Greek and a Roman.

Romanus. Si mihi de moribus Graecis narrabis, maxime delectabor. Ego quoque in studiis versor. Itaque erit mihi gratum, si disciplina puerorum Graecorum explicata erit.

Graecus. Roga : omnia explicabuntur.

Romanus. Quomodo autem tu educatus es?

PEDAGOGUE AND PUPILS. (From a terra-cotta group in the British Museum.)

Graecus. In Graeciā pueri et puellae ad septimum annum a matribus suis simul curantur.

Romanus. Ego quoque hoc modo educatus sum. Multi enim mores ex Graeciā in Italiam importati sunt.

Graecus. Tum pueri a puellis separantur. Servus fidus pueris praesidio et exemplo datur. Hic autem servus, qui paedagogus appellatur, pueros moribus bonis instituit.

Romanus. Ego quoque a servo severo curabar et docebar. Nunquam facta mea laudabantur sed semper culpabantur. Saepe a me ferula vix vitata est.

Graecus. Ad sextum decimum annum sic educatus et curatus sum. Tum mores mei satis emendati erant. Paedagogi igitur curā liberatus sum.

Romanus. Postquam prima elementa in ludo litterario memoriae mandata sunt, Vergili et Horati carmina recitabantur.

Graecus. Nos quoque Homeri carminibus ad patriae amorem incitamur, et fidibus cantare docemur.

Romanus. Quot horas in studiis quotidie versabaris?

Graecus. Mane scripta antiqua recitabantur et explicabantur. Tum praescripta duas horas retractabantur.

Romanus. Nonne corpus etiam exercebatur?

Graecus. Primo in palaestrā, deinde in gymnasio corpus exercetur et firmatur. Sic enim mens sana in corpore sano paratur.

Romanus. Verbis tuis valde delector. Bene vale!

A SEALED AND ADDRESSED LETTER, WITH TABLETS AND WRITING MATERIALS.
(From a Pompeian wall-painting and various sources.)

ROMAN MARINE VILLA. (From Pompeian wall-paintings.)

EXERCISE XXVI

PASSIVE VOICE. THIRD CONJUGATION.

INDICATIVE MOOD. PRESENT STEM.

		PRESENT.	FUTURE SIMPLE.	IMPERFECT.
		I am being ruled.	I shall be ruled.	I was being ruled.
Sing.	1.	Reg-or	Reg-ar	Reg-ēbar
	2.	Reg-eris	Reg-ēris	Reg-ēbāris
	3.	Reg-itur	Reg-ētur	Reg-ēbātur
Plur.	1.	Reg-imur	Reg-ēmur	Reg-ēbāmur
	2.	Reg-imini	Reg-ēmini	Reg-ēbāmini
	3.	Reg-untur	Reg-entur	Reg-ēbantur.

An Invitation to a Country-house.

1. Curā et sollicitudine tuā ad amorem tui maiorem adducor.
2. Tu in urbe omnibus periculis cingeris et angeris.
3. Nos in villā nostrā ab omnibus negotiis abstrahimur.
4. Neque animus neque corpus neglegetur, si huc cursus dirigetur.

5. Undique montibus cingimur et a ventis frigidis tegimur.

6. Currus saepe equis iungitur et per agros celeriter vehimur.

7. Fundus a servo meo antea male regebatur.

8. Nunc omnes res a me reguntur et administrantur.

9. Hic ab amicis veris defendēris et tegēris: in urbe ab inimicis cingeris.

10. Mora igitur non interponetur, si amore nostri adducēris.

A TWO-WHEELED CHAISE. (From a bas-relief.)

EXERCISE XXVII

DEFINITIVE PRONOUNS.

ĪDEM, 'SAME.' IPSE, 'SELF.'

Singular.

	M.	*F.*	*N.*
Nom.	Īdem	eadem	idem
Acc.	Eundem	eandem	idem
Gen.	Ēiusdem	ēiusdem	ēiusdem
Dat.	Eīdem	eīdem	eīdem
Abl.	Eōdem	eādem	eōdem.

Plural.

Nom.	Eīdem *or* Īdem	eaedem	eadem
Acc.	Eōsdem	easdem	eadem
Gen.	Eōrundem	eārundem	eōrundem
Dat.		Eīsdem *or* īsdem	
Abl.		Eīsdem *or* īsdem.	

Ipse, 'self,' is declined like **ille** (see p. 26), except in the nom. and acc. neut. singular, which ends in -**um**.

Tribute to a Friend.

1. Una domus nobis erat, idem victus, isque communis.
2. Eadem studia erant nobis ; eosdem libros legebamus.
3. Ego enim ipse cum eodem isto non invitus erravi.
4. Non omnes eadem sentimus, sed nihil audivi ex eo quod mihi ipsi molestum erat.
5. Eaedem voluntates mihi erant quae illi ipsi fuerunt.
6. Idem vultus eademque frons in hac memoriā vivunt et semper vivent.
7. Ex omnibus istis rebus, quas natura ipsa mihi dedit, nihil cum amicitiā eiusdem illius viri comparo.
8. Earundem rerum semper cupidi fuimus: unum et idem semper sentiebamus.
9. Nunquam ipse se laudabat, semper amicos suos honoribus cumulabat.
10. Mors omnibus hominibus una et eadem est. Quid autem amico fido carius esse potest ?

The definitive pronoun **ipse** must be distinguished from the reflexive **se. Ipse** may be used alone or with another pronoun or noun, but the reflexive **sē** has no nominative, and can never stand as subject, though it usually refers to the subject of its own verb.

Ipse se amat.   *He himself loves himself.*

Omne animal se ipsum diligit.   *Every animal loves itself.*

Ipse sibi inimicus est.   *He himself is hostile to himself.*

VALLUM AND FOSSA OF A FORTIFIED CAMP. (From Trajan's column and descriptions.)

· EXERCISE XXVIII

PASSIVE VOICE. THIRD CONJUGATION.

INDICATIVE MOOD.

PERFECT.	FUTURE PERFECT.	PLUPERFECT.
I have been *or* I was ruled.	I shall have been ruled.	I had been ruled.
Rectus sum.	Rectus ero.	Rectus eram.

Marius defeats the Teutons.

1. Bellum a Teutonis populo Romano indictum erat.
2. Multa verba a Mario dicta, neque a Romanis neglecta sunt.

3. 'Si imperium mihi traditum erit, bellum ad finem brevi perducetur.'

4. Tum Marius imperator electus est et copiae ex urbe ductae sunt.

5. Copiae in castris suis vallo et fossā tectae erant.

6. Tandem impetus saevus a barbaris in castra directus est.

7. Sed insidiae a Romanis post tergum barbarorum structae erant.

8. Itaque barbarorum acies iaculis et telis undique adflicta est.

9. Gens tota clade terribili destructa est.

10. Barbari enim a Romanis cincti et deleti sunt.

11. Dux Teutonorum in pugnā curru vectus erat.

12. Sed mox omnia neglecta sunt et rex ipse in fugā exstinctus est.

EXERCISE XXIX

PRONOMINAL ADJECTIVES.

ALTER, 'ONE OF TWO'; 'THE ONE,' 'THE OTHER.'
ALIUS, 'ONE,' 'ANOTHER'; *in plur.*, 'SOME,' 'OTHERS.'

Singular.

	M.	F.	N.
Nom.	Alter	Alter-a	Alter-um
Acc.	Alter-um	Alter-am	Alter-um
Gen.	Alter-ius	Alter-ius	Alter-ius
Dat.	Alter-ī	Alter-ī	Alter-ī
Abl.	Alter-ō	Alter-ā	Alter-ō.

The plural endings of alter are like those of bonus.

Singular.

	M.	*F.*	*N.*
Nom.	Ali-us	Ali-a	Ali-ud
Acc.	Ali-um	Ali-am	Ali-ud
Gen.	Al-īus	Al-īus	Al-īus
Dat.	Ali-ī	Ali-ī	Ali-ī
Abl.	Ali-ō	Ali-ā	Ali-ō

Plural.

Nom.	Ali-ī	Ali-ae	Ali-a
Acc.	Ali-ōs	Ali-ās	Ali-a
Gen.	Ali-ōrum	Ali-ārum	Ali-ōrum
Dat. and Abl.	Ali-īs	Ali-īs	Ali-īs.

JULIUS CAESAR. (From the bust in the British Museum.)

Caesar and Pompey.

1. Erant Romanā in civitate duae factiones, quarum altera Caesaris causam, altera Pompei agebat.
2. Neque alter ex his ducibus alteri cedebat.
3. Romanorum alii alterum, alterum alii adiuvabant.
4. Alios divitiae, alios gloriae cupido ad arma incitabant.

5. Alterius ducis natura semper magna, alterius saepe turpissima erat.

6. In pugnā ad Pharsalum (id vico nomen fuit), legiones aliae in alia parte pugnabant.

7. Alius alii auxilium praebet : alius alio more pugnat.

8. In hac pugnā res aliae secundae, aliae adversae Caesari fuerunt.

9. Tandem Pompeius cum paucis aliis in navem properavit.

10. Mox duces, alter a sicariis in Aegypto, alter a civibus in urbe Romā, trucidati sunt.

POMPEY.
(From the bust in the Naples Museum.)

Alter can only refer to two people or parties. **Alter,** 'the one'; **alter,** 'the other.' **Alius** refers to any number of people.

Alii fossis, alii vallo, alii turribus castra muniebant.
Some fortified the camp with ditches, others with a rampart, others with towers.

Alius repeated with a different case means 'one another'; 'some one . . . some another.'

Alius alio more vivit. *Some men live in one way, some in another.*

ANCIENT BRITONS.

EXERCISE XXX

PASSIVE VOICE. FOURTH CONJUGATION.

		PRESENT.	FUTURE SIMPLE.	IMPERFECT.
		I am heard.	I shall be heard.	I was being heard.
Sing.	1.	Aud-ior	Aud-iar	Aud-iēbar
	2.	Aud-īris	Aud-iēris	Aud-iēbāris
	3.	Aud-ītur	Aud-iētur	Aud-iēbātur
Plur.	1.	Aud-īmur	Aud-iēmur	Aud-iēbāmur
	2.	Aud-īmini	Aud-iēmini	Aud-iēbāmini
	3.	Aud-iuntur	Aud-ientur	Aud-iēbantur.

A Letter from a Roman in Britain. B.C. 54.

1. Bellum in hac terrā horridā et barbarā mox finietur.
2. Ego quotidie multis et magnis laboribus a scribendo impedior.
3. Quomodo autem tu a promissis tuis impediris?
4. Hodie omne opus expeditur et mala mea finiuntur.
5. Nihil argenti in insulā reperitur.
6. Multi servi in castris custodiuntur, litteris autem Britanni male erudiuntur.
7. Nos semper lino aut lanis vestimur, sed barbari pellibus vestiuntur.
8. Nos frumento nutrimur: illi carne et lacte nutriuntur.
9. Aditus insulae magnis molibus muniebantur.
10. Insula his operibus ab incursionibus custodiebatur.
11. Ira mea tempore lenitur et mollitur.
12. Pax autem tecum non expedietur, nisi epistola mittetur.

ROMANS STORMING A BRITISH STRONGHOLD.
(Adapted from Trajan's column.)

EXERCISE XXXI

PERFECT.	FUTURE PERFECT.	PLUPERFECT.
I have been heard.	I shall have been heard.	I had been heard.
Audītus sum.	Audītus ero.	Audītus eram.

Defeat of Cassivellaunus, a British Chief.

1. Cassivellauni oppidum silvis et paludibus munitum est.
2. Itaque Caesaris agmen undique impeditum erat.
3. Iter magno cum labore a Caesare expeditum est.
4. Locus naturā et opere munitus et impeditus est.
5. Militum labores victoriā magnā sunt finiti.
6. Caesaris ira hostium doloribus mollita et lenita est.
7. 'Nisi fraude impeditus ero, non puniemini.'
8. 'Si castra iterum munita erunt, poenas gravissimas dabitis.'
9. Strepitus feminarum et liberorum auditus est.
10. Sed bellum finitum, et res expedita est.

EXERCISE XXXII

DEMONSTRATIVE, INTERROGATIVE AND RELATIVE PRONOUNS.

Visit to a Roman House.

Augustus. Cuius est haec domus?

Claudius. Quā de causā id rogas?

Augustus. Hāc nunquam domum splendidiorem vidi.

Claudius. Unus ex amicis meis hanc domum custodit. Pulsa! Eam visemus.

Custos. Quis adest?

Claudius. Claudius sum. Salve!

Custos. Salve multum! Quam ob causam ades?

Claudius. Nonne huic meo comiti hanc domum aperies?

Custos. Nonne eam iam saepe spectavisti?

Claudius. Ego iam eandem spectavi, sed hic meus amicus advena est.

Custos. Morem ei libenter geram. Primum hoc est vestibulum. Spectate hanc portam splendidam!

Claudius. Quam bene figura canis in isto limine est picta!

Augustus. Specta quoque haec verba, quibus mendici terrentur.—'Cave canem!'

Custos. Huic proximum est atrii ostium, quod servus ille semper custodit.

Augustus. Quam splendidum est illud atrium! Quam pulchris tabulis est ornatum!

Claudius. Quae autem sunt fabulae in his tabulis?

Custos. In hāc tabulā Ulixes Polyphemum caecat, in illā Aeneas in Italiam navigat.

PERISTYLE OF A HOUSE AT POMPEII.

Brogi photo.]

E 2

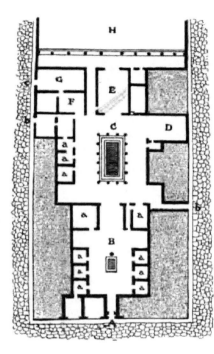

GROUND PLAN OF A ROMAN
HOUSE. (The house of Pansa,
Pompeii.)

A. The front door.
B. The atrium with the impluvium and altar in centre.
C. Peristylium with piscina in centre.
D. Triclinium or dining-room.
E. Œcus.
F. Kitchen.
G. Courtyard.
H. Garden.
a a a a. Chambers.
b b. Entrances from side streets.
c. Servants' entrance.

EXERCISE XXXIII

PRONOUNS.

Visit to a Roman House (continued).

Custos. Hoc spatium apertum in medio atrio est impluvium.

Claudius. Quam bene signis et columnis cinctum et ornatum est!

Custos. Hoc cubiculum in dextrā est domino proprium. Illud est tabulinum, ubi negotium a domino administratur.

Claudius. Quid pulchrius esse potest illo solo marmoreo?

Custos. Per has fauces in peristylium intrabimus, quod columnis marmoreis est cinctum. In medio est piscina; in dextrā est triclinium.

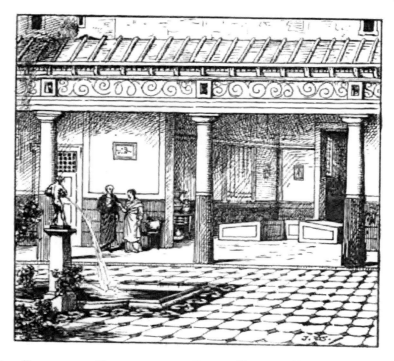

The Piscina and Triclinium of a Roman House. (From restorations of a Pompeian house.)

Claudius. Quae fenestrae splendidae! Qui colores! Quae signa! Quid narrat caecus ille?

Custos. Ille est Homerus, qui Helenae dicit, ' Quae male tu egisti, ego bene cantavi.'

Augustus. Ecce color harum fenestrarum! Quo spectant illae fenestrae?

Custos. Hae in hortum, illae in viam. Iam omnia vidisti. Hoc est posticum.

Augustus. Tibi maximas gratias ago. Vale.

Custos. Bene valete et vivite!

Claudius. Quod huic par est spectaculum?

EXERCISE XXXIV

IRREGULAR VERBS.

VOLO, NŌLO, MĀLO.

INDICATIVE PRESENT.

	I am willing *or* I wish.	I am unwilling, do not wish, refuse.	I wish rather, prefer.
Sing. 1.	Volo	Nōlo	Mălo
2.	Vīs	Nonvisᶜ	Măvis
3.	Vult	Nonvult	Mavult
Plur. 1.	Volumus	Nōlumus	Mălumus
2.	Vultis	Nonvultis	Mavultis
3.	Volunt	Nōlunt	Mālunt.

The other tenses in the Indicative follow the Third Conjugation.

FUTURE SIMPLE.	IMPERFECT.	PERFECT.
Volam	Volēbam	Volui
Nōlam	Nōlebam	Nōlui
Mălam	Mălebam	Mălui.

Nolo alone has an imperative:

    2nd Sing. Nōlī.   *2nd Plur.* Nōlīte.

Inauguration of the Australian Commonwealth. A.D. 1901.

Britannus 1. In Australiam navigare volumus. Nonne tu nobiscum venire vis?

Britannus 2. Eadem, quae tu vis, ego volo; sed frustra.

Britannus 1. Si fortuna volet, et ipse voles, cur venire noles?

Britannus 2. Eas regiones videre semper volui, sed uxor mea nonvult.

Britannus 1. Nonne iudicio tuo quam aliorum stare mavis? Nolent, ubi voles; ubi noles, volent.

Britannus 2. Noli hoc putare; Australiam enim uxor non visere noluit, sed Canadam videre vult.

Britannus 1. Sed vir et uxor, si in amicitiā manere volent, semper idem volent et idem nolent.

Britannus 2. Ego tamen servire quam pugnare malo. Non iam eadem senex vult quae puer voluit.

Britannus 1. Rem seriam tecum agere volo. Si proximo anno in Canadam navigare volueris, nonne hoc anno uxor tua Australiam visere volet?

Britannus 2. Cur autem Australiam hoc anno quam proximo videre mavis?

Britannus 1. Quia hoc anno cives omnium civitatum in Australiā foedus et societatem iungunt. Exordium rei-publicae videre volumus.

Britannus 2. Ego quoque adesse volam. Adero, si potero.

Britannus 1. Si volueris, gratias tibi agam. Si nolueris veniam nunquam impetrabis. Noli spem destituere!

Nolo is compounded of **non** and **volo**; **malo** of **magis** and **volo**.

Prolative Infinitive. These three verbs, like other verbs of wishing, are often followed by an infinitive to carry on the sense and complete the sentence; as Volo ire, *I wish to go.*

Prohibition. The imperative noli followed by a present infinitive is the usual way of expressing a prohibition.

Noli putare. *Do not think.*

BRAILING THE SAIL. (From a Pompeian grave-relief.)

EXERCISE XXXV

THE VERB ĪRE, 'To Go', AND ITS COMPOUNDS.

	PRESENT	FUTURE SIMPLE.	IMPERFECT.
Sing. 1.	Eo	Ī-bo	Ī-bam
2.	Īs	Ī-bis	Ī-băs
3.	It	Ī-bit	Ī-băt
Plur. 1.	Īmus	Ī-bimus	Ī-bămus
2.	Ītis	Ī-bitis	Ī-bătis
3.	Eunt	Ī-bunt	Ī-bant.

The perfect stem ii is conjugated regularly, but in the simple verb a longer form īvi is sometimes found.

IMPERATIVE PRESENT: Ī, 'Go thou'; Īte, 'Go ye.'

A Journey from Brundisium to Rome.

Marcus. Salve! Quando Brundisio Romam rediisti?

Quintus. Abhinc tres dies. Totum annum Brundisi fui.

Marcus. Ego Romae totam aestatem fui. Quid narras de itinere tuo?

Quintus. Brundisio Neapolim equo vectus sum. Deinde Neapoli Romam feliciter navigavi.

Brogi photo.]

THE BAY OF NAPLES.

Marcus. Quando Brundisium Romā redibis?

Quintus. Ubi frater meus Carthagine redierit, statim iter inibimus.

Marcus. Quo autem ibis? Num illuc redibis, unde abiisti?

Quintus. Non statim Brundisium redibimus. Paulisper Baiis manebimus.

Marcus. Multos abhinc annos Neapoli habitabam. Quomodo res ibi et Puteolis nunc se habent?

Quintus. Nunquam Neapolim ivimus. Locus turbulentus est et Graecis plenus. Baiis autem et Puteolis est vita semper iucunda et tranquilla.

Marcus. Nihil de itinere tuo narravisti.

Quintus. Necesse est domum redire. Cras, si in thermas adibis, omnia tibi narrabo.

Marcus. Domi ad sextam horam ero. Tum in thermas prodibo. I domum et vale!

Names of Towns and Small Islands.

Rules of Place. With names of towns or small islands, **Place where? Whither?** or **Whence?** is expressed by the **Case without a Preposition.**

(1) **Place where?** is expressed by the Ablative, except the Substantive be of the First or Second Declension and Singular Number, when it is expressed by the Genitive.

Genitive. 1st and 2nd Decl. Sing.

Marcus Romae, Quintus Brundisi est.
Marcus is at Rome, Quintus at Brundisium.

Ablative. 1st and 2nd Decl. Plur.

Marcus Baiis, Quintus Puteolis est.
Marcus is at Baiae, Quintus at Puteoli.

Ablative. 3rd Decl. Sing. or Plur.

Marcus Neapoli, Quintus Gadibus est.
Marcus is at Naples, Quintus at Gades.

(2) **Place whither?** is expressed by the Accusative, and **Place whence?** by the Ablative, without Prepositions.

Romam, *to Rome*; Baias, *to Baiae*.
Brundisium, *to Brundisium*; Puteolos, *to Puteoli*.
Neapolim, *to Naples*; Gades, *to Gades*.

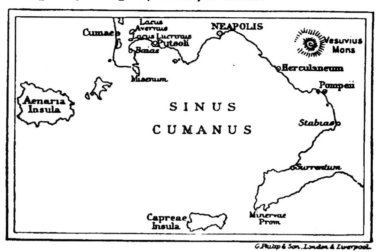

G.Philip & Son. London & Liverpool.

Roma, *from Rome*; Baiis, *from Baiae*.
Carthagine, *from Carthage*; Puteolis, *from Puteoli*.

The Substantives domus and rus are similarly used.
Domi, *at home*   domum, *homewards*   domo, *from home*.
Ruri, *in the country*   rus, *to the country*   rure, *from the country*.

EXERCISE XXXVI

A Journey from Brundisium to Rome (continued).

Marcus. Salve! Ad tempus venisti.

Quintus. Quot homines ineunt et exeunt! Qui strepitus est!

Marcus. Multi domum mox redibunt. Locus iam nobis est.

Quintus. Magnopere gaudeo quod rure redii. Quomodo res domi se habent?

Marcus. Bene se habent. Quid autem ruri agebas?

Quintus. Brundisi (id quod tibi iam notum est) diu

fueram. Domi erat Caesar, amicus meus, quocum habitabam. Necesse erat negoti causā Romam adire.

Marcus. Nonne Brundisio cum Gaio exiisti?

Quintus. Unā cum Gaio Beneventum properavi. Imber in itinere toto semper gravis et molestus erat.

Marcus. Ego Beneventi diu habitabam. Panis ater est et durus semper.

Quintus. Benevento Capuam pedibus iimus. Capuae caupo noster, dum cenam parat, tectum paene incendit.

Marcus. Abi, ludis me. Tu, qui Romā severus abiisti, iocosus domum redis.

Quintus. Melius est incendium quam cena frigida.

Marcus. Quomodo Neapolim Capuā adiisti?

Quintus. Tres dies Pompeiis egi. Hinc viā pulcherrimā Baias adii. Amicus meus Puteolis manet. Ego Baiis navem conscendi et feliciter Romam redii.

EXERCISE XXXVII

VERBS IN -IO OF THE THIRD CONJUGATION.

ACTIVE VOICE.	PASSIVE VOICE.
PRESENT TENSE.	PRESENT TENSE.
I take.	I am taken.

Sing.	1. Capi-o	Capi-or
	2. Cap-is	Cap-eris
	3. Cap-it	Cap-itur
Plur.	1. Cap-imus	Cap-imur
	2. Cap-itis	Cap-imini
	3. Capi-unt	(Capi-untur.)

FUTURE SIMPLE.	FUTURE SIMPLE.
Capi-am	Cap-iar.

IMPERFECT.	IMPERFECT.
Capi-ēbam	Cap-iēbar.

PRESENT IMPERATIVE ACTIVE.

Cap-e, 'take thou.'   Capi-te, 'take ye.'

HANNIBAL'S ELEPHANTS.   (From an engraved gem.)

The Carthaginians invade Italy.

1. Dum Poeni in Italiam iter faciunt, magnus terror Romanos capiebat.

2. Tandem Hannibal exercitum suum Alpes traicit et locum castris aptum capit.

3. Mox multae et magnae clades a Romanis accipiuntur; cives omni spe salutis deiciuntur.

4. Hannibal Romam iter non faciebat sed apud vicum Cannas locum castris aptum rapiebat.

5. Subito Romani in castra Poenorum impetum faciunt.

6. Romani autem maximam cladem accipiunt et undique fugiunt.

7. Consul a militibus in fugā rapitur; frustra verba facit:

8. 'Quo fugitis, milites?   Quo me rapietis?'

9. 'Nisi arma capietis et impetum in hostes facietis, magna clades accipietur.'

10. Poeni quattuor milia Romanorum capiunt, magnam praedam faciunt.

EXERCISE XXXVIII

DEPONENT VERBS.

Deponent verbs are passive in form, that is, they are conjugated like Passives, but are active in meaning, and most of them are transitive. Examples:—

1st Conjugation.	Imitor, *I imitate.*	-āri, -ātus sum.
2nd Conjugation.	Mereor, *I deserve.*	-ēri, -itus sum.
3rd Conjugation.	Ūtor, *I use.*	-i, ūsus sum.
„ (like capior).	Patior, *I suffer.*	-i, passus sum.
4th Conjugation.	Largior, *I bestow.*	-īri, -ītus sum.

Death of Queen Victoria, Jan. 22nd, 1901.

Regina nostra, postquam sexaginta tres annos imperium maximum optime moderata est, plena annis, plena honoribus mortua est.

O triste funus! Sed, quamquam unus dies tot spes, tot gaudia frustratus est, nos eius exemplum imitari conabimur. Nam si Deus non tam precibus quam probitate et virtute laetatur, nonne regina his rebus summos honores merita est?

Semper illum triumphum recordabimur, ubi tot reges principesque reginam nostram ad templum Dei comitati sunt. Gloria autem virtutem sequitur: gloria probitatem comitatur et semper comitabitur. Omnes igitur boni reginae probitatem aemulabuntur; omnes virtutem non solum admirabuntur sed etiam imitabuntur. Non enim pro se sed pro populo semper nitebatur domina nostra, et cum civibus suis omnes dolores, gaudia omnia partiebatur.

Ab his initiis amor noster proficiscitur; has ob causas reginam beatam veneramur. Nos etiam, quia illius praeclarum praeceptum sequi et imitari semper studebimus, diem, quo mortua est, summā religione venerabimur.

ULYSSES ARRIVING AT THE ISLAND OF CYCLOPS.
(From Greek vase paintings.)

EXERCISE XXXIX

RECAPITULATORY EXERCISES

Cyclops complains to his father Neptune about Ulysses.

Cyclops. Pater, da mihi auxilium! Magno dolore compleor, quia ab hospite improbo male tractatus sum.

Neptune. Quomodo autem hoc scelus paratum est?

Cyclops. Vinum validum mihi datum erat. Tum somno gravi oppressus, a barbaro superatus et caecatus sum.

Neptune. Si alios contempseris, ab aliis contemnēris. Nonne te ipsum defendere potuisti?

Cyclops. Dolus a barbaro adhibitus est. Consilia callida callidis verbis tecta erant. Omnia a me sunt neglecta.

Neptune. Multa semper ignorabis, nisi exemplo meo doceberis. Dic mihi! A quo hoc facinus commissum est?

Cyclops. Navis barbara ad insulam meam ventis adversis pulsa est cuius magistro nomen erat Nemo. Postea autem, dum ex portu exit, Nemo ab amicis suis Ulixes appellabatur.

Neptune. Iste Graecus mihi notus est. Multos annos circa moenia Troiana pugnavit. Idem iam multos annos oceanum pererrat. Delectabor si de consilio callido me certiorem feceris.

EXERCISE XL

Complaint of Cyclops (continued).

Cyclops. Postquam oves meae ex agris in speluncam reductae sunt, ignis a me accendebatur. Tum barbari in ultimā speluncā conspecti sunt. Alii aliā in parte se celare conabantur. Statim duo Graeci a me raptati et devorati sunt.

Neptune. Ut rexeris, ita regēris. Quomodo autem ceteri Graeci e spelunca fugerunt?

Cyclops. Ubi Nemo vinum dulce mihi dedit, somno gravi statim oppressus sum. Dum somno vincior, oculus mihi ereptus est.

Neptune. Eheu! Quam graviter somno oppressus es, fili! Mirum est quod e somno non excitatus es. Cur autem comites tui subsidio non venerunt?

Cyclops. Nempe clamoribus meis excitati sunt. Tum me rogaverunt: 'A quo oppugnaris?' 'Nemo me oppugnat,' ego responsum dedi. Sic a comitibus furore plenis desertus sum.

Neptune. Bono animo es, fili! Antequam Ulixes in Graeciam venerit, maximas poenas tibi dabit.

ENGLISH EXERCISES

I. CARDINAL NUMERALS.

1. The Romans used to have many gods, we have one God.

2. The world is the work of one God, not of many.

3. Nature gives to one man two feet, two hands, two knees.

4. To one man there is one head, but to Cerberus there were three heads.

5. The three Graces or goddesses of beauty were dear to the Greek poets.

6. Spring, summer, autumn, winter are the four seasons of one year.

7. A man has five senses of the body.

8. Six days out of seven are sacred to work.

9. Out of seven days one day is sacred to God.

10. Rome had seven kings and seven hills.

˜, ⁄ᴍ. 6. Julius Caesar called the seventh month by his own name.

ᴍ . ᴃ 7. Augustus, the first emperor of the Romans, changed the name of the eighth month.

'+ .ᴘ. 8. When (*ubi*) March was the first month of the year, then September was the seventh.

ᴋ´ ꜰ 9. October was the eighth month, November the ninth (month), December the tenth of the Roman year.

ꜰ .ᴍ. 10. December, the twelfth month, no longer has a suitable name.

(ˎ ʋ)

IV. CARDINAL AND ORDINAL NUMERALS.

Seven Wonders of the World.

ᴋ ꜰ 1. The tomb of the Egyptian king was four hundred feet high and seven hundred feet broad.

ᴋ ꜰ 2. One hundred thousand slaves prepared the tomb.

ᴍ 3. The tomb of Mausolus was one hundred and forty feet high.

4. A chariot, fifty-two feet high, adorned the monument.

5. One hundred and thirty columns adorned the temple of Diana.

6. The temple was one hundred and twenty feet high.

7. A statue of Apollo, one hundred and twenty-one feet high, adorned the entrance of the harbour.

8. An immense statue of Jupiter used to stand in the Olympian temple.

9. The famous statue was the work of Phidias.

10. The tombs of Egypt alone remain out of the seven wonders.

V.

1. The Roman people were under kings during two hundred and forty-four years.
2. In the battle of Cannae (*adj.*) the Carthaginians killed fifteen thousand Romans.
3. In the Persian war Xerxes sailed to Greece with twelve hundred ships.
4. The land forces were seven hundred thousand foot-soldiers, forty thousand horse-soldiers.
5. Nine thousand Athenians defeated a hundred thousand foot-soldiers, ten thousand horse-soldiers in the battle of Marathon (*adj.*).
6. The plain of Marathon is distant ten thousand paces from the town.
7. At (*apud*) Plataea a few Greeks routed two hundred thousand foot-soldiers, twenty thousand horse-soldiers.
8. Alexander led into Asia thirty thousand infantry, four thousand five hundred cavalry.

VI. INFINITIVE MOOD. PRESENT TENSE.

A few sayings of the Ancients.

1. It is pleasant to have many friends.
2. No one is able to avoid death.
3. It is dangerous to attack an enemy without arms.
4. It is disgraceful to overcome an adversary by fraud.
5. If it shall be necessary to hasten flight in war, it will be useful to exercise the feet before the battle.

6. We are all able to fight for our country.
7. It is pleasant in summer to lie under a tree.
8. It is difficult to rule bad boys.
9. All good citizens are able to keep the laws of their country.
10. All men are able to speak : you are not all able to listen.

VII. PRESENT TENSE (*continued*).

A few more sayings.

1. It is the nature of boys to love games, to avoid work.
2. It is difficult to keep everything in-memory.
3. It is the nature of sailors to love the sea; it is the duty of farmers to plough the fields.
4. It is the duty of good citizens to keep the laws of the republic.
5. It is the duty of a father to punish and to train his boys.
6. It is the nature of barbarians to destroy temples.
7. You will not be able to be present unless I shall have been able to lend you help.
8. All have been able to blame, few will be able to praise you.
9. It is never useful to sin; it is always easy to err.
10. To fight is not sufficient: it is necessary always to gain the victory.

VIII. COMPARISON OF ADJECTIVES.

Socrates.

1. We have already heard about Socrates, the **most** famous philosopher and most prudent **man.**
2. The integrity of his-most honourable life was **very** well known (*superl.*) to all the Athenians.
3. The most excellent citizen and most learned philosopher was not more eager of money than **of** glory.
4. Socrates, the wisest of all the Athenians, spent **a** most holy life.
5. He was worthy of the most ample honours, but **the** citizens punished the most innocent **hero** with a most disgraceful death.
6. No one ever awaited death with a firmer mind.
7. Few speeches are more celebrated than the **last** speech of the philosopher.
8. To his friends he was most pleasant, to all **tyrants** most hostile.
9. Nothing is more excellent, nothing firmer than the example of the most honourable philosopher.
10. The tyrants never devised a baser crime than **the** death (*abl.*) of Socrates.

IX. IMPERATIVE MOOD. PRESENT TENSE.

Dialogue at a Banquet.

Guest 1. Hasten your course ! We shall never be **present** in time.

Guest 2. Take care, my friends ! We have wandered from the way.

Guest 3. Come hither, boys ! Show us the way to the temple of Vesta.

Boy 1. Direct your course through the gardens of Caesar! Then bend to the left! If you shall then be uncertain, ask again!

Guest 4. Be thou our guide! Lead us and show us the way! There will be a reward for thee.

Guest 1. Lead us to the temple! Lend aid to us!

Boy 2. Behold the temple of Vesta! Farewell!

Guest 2. Stay a little! Give me thy hand! Take (hold) thy reward!

Boy 2. Keep thy money! The work is not worthy of a reward.

Guest 4. We are grateful to thee. Farewell all!

Guest 1. Call the slave! Knock at the door!

X. PRESENT TENSE (*continued*).

Guest 1. Give pardon to us, if we have arrived late. We wandered from the way.

Host. Good-day, friends! Give your cloaks to the slave!

Guest 2. Take care, boy! Hold my cloak with care!

Host. Lead us to the triclinium! The way is known to you!

Guest 3. Look, my friend, at the beautiful pictures!

Guest 4. Relate to me your story!

Host. Keep the tale and tell (it) at dessert! Come! Choose your couches! Recline, my friends! Take away the sandals, slaves!

Guest 1. Recline near me and delight me with your witty conversation!

Host. Bring, slaves, olives and chestnuts!

Guest 2. Enough of fruit. Mix and give me a goblet!

Host. Fill up the goblets with wine! Give us the sandals, slaves! Remove the table!

XI. IRREGULAR COMPARISON OF ADJECTIVES.

Alexander the Great.

1. No one out of all the Greeks was greater or braver than Alexander.

2. In greater and in smaller matters he always showed very great zeal.

3. He looked after the greatest matters, and did not neglect the smallest affairs.

4. The king always thought nature a better guide than very many men.

5. He won more victories by courage and strategy than by the number of his soldiers.

6. The king was greater and more distinguished in the arts of war than of peace.

7. The mind of the king was always preparing greater and better designs.

8. The soldiers thought the anger of Alexander a greater punishment than death.

9. If Alexander was very inclined to anger, he was more inclined to sorrow.

10. And so the death of Clitus was a source of very great grief (*dat.*) to Alexander.

XII. PASSIVE VOICE.

FIRST CONJUGATION. PRESENT AND FUTURE.

A General exhorts his Troops.

1. After an unsuccessful battle the soldiers are called together by the general.

2. The timid legions are thus urged on to the fight.

3. 'Why, my friends, are we so disturbed by our disaster?'

4. 'Our fields are being laid waste by the enemy; our towns are being attacked.'

5. 'The barbarians will soon be overcome and put to flight by you.'

6. 'I am neither disturbed by the number nor am I distressed by the courage of the enemy.'

7. 'But I shall be tortured with very great grief, if we shall again be routed.'

8. 'The city will never be stormed, if your courage shall be aroused by my words.'

9. 'A victory will be gained: we shall be loaded with many honours by the citizens.'

10. 'Courage is demanded: courage will not be expected in vain.'

XIII. IMPERFECT TENSE.

Frugality in Ancient Rome.

1. Honest customs were preserved for a long time by the ancient Romans.

2. The boys were educated according to (*ad*) strict rules.

3. Frugality was praised; luxury was condemned by the masters.

4. The minds of the pupils were urged on thus by good advice.

5. 'If the example of your fathers shall be kept, you will be loaded with honours.'

6. 'Your fathers were educated thus: the good examples will be kept by you.'

7. 'They were loved and praised by all good men.'

8. 'You will be loved by many, if a good example shall be set (given) by you.'

9. 'If the old customs shall be changed, the republic will not be strengthened.'

10. But the words of the leaders were avoided; the customs were changed.

XIV. DEMONSTRATIVE PRONOUN.

IS. 'That'; 'He,' 'She,' 'It.'

Alexander in Asia.

1. When those affairs were reported, Alexander called together his generals.
2. Then with fierce words he urged on their minds to battle.
3. 'You have overcome the enemy and stormed their camp.'
4. 'You have defeated them in battle ; you have routed their cavalry.'
5. 'But you have overcome neither their spirit nor their courage.'
6. 'Many brave men have been killed, but more are awaiting us.'
7. 'You have laid waste their fields : you have driven them from their towns.'
8. 'But those disasters are neither a hindrance nor care to them.'
9. 'They are fighting for their country and their altars : you have not yet frightened them.'
10. 'Prepare yourselves for battle : we will gain a final victory over (*ab*) them.'

XV. PERFECT TENSES.

Frugality at Rome.

CINCINNATUS, CURIUS AND FABRICIUS.

1. The sons of Brutus were condemned to death by their own father.
2. Camillus and Fabricius had been tempted in vain with money by the enemy.
3. A rustic life was loved by Camillus; luxury had been avoided by him.
4. The simple hero was called from the plough to the dictatorship.
5. The state had been saved; the enemy had been routed.
6. But the humble life was not changed.
7. A rustic life was valued more highly than riches.
8. By their good examples we have been urged on to a noble life.
9. But we were surpassed by the ancients in frugality and virtue.
10. If our customs shall be changed, their example will not have been praised in vain.

XVI. PARTITIVE GENITIVE AFTER ADVERBS AND NEUTER ADJECTIVES.

Decline of Roman Morals.

1. Before the Carthaginian war the Romans had much moderation, little avarice.
2. Then all the leaders desired more wealth and exercised less virtue.
3. Soon there was much authority in the hands of the senators, little in the hands of the consuls.
4. And so the republic had not sufficient strength.
5. The citizens wanted very much pleasure, the senators very much riches.

6. And so the magistrates gave much corn and games to the citizens without payment.

7. Soon the senators had much power, the consuls had no authority.

8. Everywhere there was too much plotting, too little honesty and virtue.

9. At last there was no honesty, no frugality in the city of Rome.

10. The republic, because it had not sufficient protection, was overcome by its enemies.

XVII. ACTIVE AND PASSIVE TENSES.

Dialogue between the Ghosts of Xerxes and Leonidas.

Xerxes. A great honour has been given to you by me.

Leonidas. Neither glory nor honour is desired by me.

Xerxes. Thou alone shall be appointed attendant of the Great King.

Leonidas. I do not desire the honour. I am tortured with grief, because I have not avoided thee by my death.

Xerxes. What! How shall the Great King be compared with the leader of a few robbers?

Leonidas. Not by courage but by number didst thou overcome us.

Xerxes. Was not the sea laden with my ships, the land filled by my soldiers?

Leonidas. We were only overcome because we were tired by slaughter.

Xerxes. I shall always be tortured with grief, because your country was not laid waste by me.

Leonidas. Neither by your insults nor by your praise shall I be excited. Minos, the judge of the dead, awaits you. Farewell!

XVIII. DEMONSTRATIVE PRONOUNS.

HIC, 'THIS' (NEAR ME), *or* 'HE, 'SHE,' 'IT'; 'THE LATTER.'

ILLE, 'THAT' (YONDER), *or* 'HE, 'SHE,' 'IT'; 'THE FORMER.'

Philip and Alexander.

1. The great and famous (*Magnus ille*) Alexander surpassed his father Philip both in virtue and in vices.

2. The citizens obeyed the former through love, the latter through fear.

3. The plans of the former were more prudent, the mind of the latter more splendid.

4. Rage was often concealed by the latter, never by the former.

5. And so that sad death of the faithful Clitus is an object of disgrace to the former.

6. By these arts the father prepared a mighty kingdom, by those plans the son finished the glory of that work.

7. Yet the deeds of these kings were not a means of safety (*pred. dat.*) to their state.

8. The former was overcome by the sword of the assassin, the latter by the vices of youth.

9. Those words also of the famous orator are worthy of recollection:

10. 'The former was always Great, the latter often most base.'

XIX. SECOND CONJUGATION.

INDICATIVE MOOD. PRESENT STEM.

Dialogue between the Ghosts of Achilles and Homer.

Achilles. My mind is filled with joy, because a splendid tale is provided for you by my deeds.

Homer. Thanks will be due to Ulysses more than to you.

Achilles. What ! Is not more praise due to my courage than to his cunning ?

Homer. The fame of my songs will be increased more by the deeds of the wise Ulysses than the fierce Achilles.

Achilles. Ungrateful poet, you are moved by vain anger.

Homer. I shall not be frightened by the anger of a shade. No longer is a sword held by your right-hand.

Achilles. Your fame is due to me but now I am attacked by ungrateful words.

Homer. You are filled with pride and will not be taught by good advice.

Achilles. Formerly the Trojans were terrified by my deeds. Now I am not feared by an ungrateful poet.

Homer. If my poems shall be destroyed, your name will no longer be held in-memory.

Achilles. In vain you wilt be advised by my words: soon you will be taught by hard example.

XX. INTERROGATIVE PRONOUN. QUIS, 'WHO ?'

Dialogue between Alexander the Great and a Scythian Chief.

Scythian. On account of what reasons dost thou approach our country with an army ?

Alexander. What barbarian attacks me with these words ? To what tribes is the name of Alexander not known?

Scythian. On what terms wilt thou grant peace to us ? To whom is not his native-land most dear ?

Alexander. With what gifts wilt thou appease my soldiers? To whom will Alexander refuse friendship?

Scythian. What friendship can there be between Greeks and Scythians?

Alexander. To what tribes have I not given fair terms? What examples dost thou fear?

Scythian. With what victories wilt thou be content? Of what lands art thou not covetous?

Alexander. What better friend is there than Alexander?

Scythian. What greater robber have we ever beheld?

Alexander. What cities have I not stormed? Who will attack Alexander?

Scythian. Farewell. Fortune will help the better cause.

XXI. SECOND CONJUGATION. PERFECT STEM.

Battle of Cannae. B.C. 216.

1. The Romans were terrified with fear, for two armies had been destroyed by the Carthaginians.
2. The citizens were scarcely prevented from flight.
3. All were deterred by fear from good counsels.
4. Confidence was no longer placed (*habeo*) in-the-generals (*dat.*).
5. The courage of the soldiers was destroyed by disasters.
6. Then Hannibal was advised with fierce words.
7. 'The city will soon be destroyed, if the fortifications shall be at once besieged.'
8. 'With difficulty have the Roman soldiers been deterred from flight.'
9. But Hannibal was held back by vain fear.
10. In vain he was warned; the legions were kept (*habeo*) in camp; the walls were not besieged.

XXII. RELATIVE PRONOUN.

QUI, 'WHO,' 'WHICH.'

Story of Carthage. First Punic War. B. C. 264–241.

1. The Tyrians, who lived in Asia, settled colonies in many places.
2. Out of those colonies, which the Tyrians settled in Africa, Carthage was most famous.
3. The Carthaginians, whose fleet was very large, soon crossed over to Sicily.
4. Soon the Roman people brought about a war, which was destructive to the Carthaginians.
5. In Sicily the Romans, whose army was very powerful, overcame the Carthaginians.
6. But at sea the Carthaginian fleet, in-which the barbarians were superior, was victorious.
7. At last the Romans built many ships, with which they attacked the barbarians.
8. At first the consul, who was leading the fleet, gained a great victory.
9. But soon the general, whom the Romans appointed in his place, was severely defeated.
10. Then the Romans, whose courage was tired but not overcome, prepared a new fleet.

XXIII. *Second Punic War.* B. C. 218–201.

1. Out of all the wars, which the Roman people ever waged, the second Punic war is most worthy of mention.

2. Hannibal, whom the Carthaginians elected general, led the army with great boldness.

3. Soon he led the forces, which he had with him in Spain, through the Alps into Italy.

4. Scipio, who was awaiting the arrival of Hannibal, prepared his forces for battle.

5. But the enemy, who were superior in cavalry, easily defeated the consul.

6. The Romans, whom many disasters seriously frightened, elected a dictator.

7. But his plans, which had been most expedient, did not please the people.

8. And so the consuls, to whom large forces had been given, attacked the Carthaginian camp.

9. In the battle of Cannae, of which we have already heard, the Romans were overcome and routed.

10. At last Hannibal, whose soldiers were worn out by many labours, sailed for Africa.

XXIV. RELATIVE PRONOUN.

Third Punic War. B.C. 146.

1. After many years the Romans, who still feared the Carthaginians, renewed the war.

2. Ambassadors, whom the senate sent to Africa, rejected the terms of peace.

3. Then the senate declared war on the Carthaginians, whose army was no longer a match for the Romans.

4. At length Carthage, which had been besieged for three years, was stormed.

5. The buildings, which the citizens had **raised with** great pride, were levelled with-the-ground.
6. Scipio, whose grandfather had been **defeated by** Hannibal, destroyed the town.
7. The Romans gave to the conqueror the cognomen which his grandfather had had.
8. And so the Carthaginians, with whom the Romans had waged war for a hundred and twenty years, were overcome and blotted out.

XXV. FIRST AND SECOND CONJUGATIONS.

PASSIVE INDICATIVE.

Dialogue between a Greek and a Roman.

Greek. How are boys educated in your native-land?

Roman. First we are taught in an elementary school.

Greek. When the first elements shall have been explained, what is then handled?

Roman. The letters were formed by the master, then they were copied by us.

Greek. Soon you were able to read and write. Were not the words of the poets then recited?

Roman. We were often delighted with the poems of Homer.

Greek. While his beautiful writings were being recited (*pres.*), were you not also delighted by music?

Roman. We were then taught to sing to the lyre (*abl.*).

Greek. How was the lyre handled by you?

Roman. It was held by the left-hand and struck with the right.

Greek. While the mind was being strengthened by study, was not the body also exercised?

Roman. Our limbs were exercised daily in the gymnasium.

Greek. When were you released from the care of your preceptor?

Roman. After sixteen years had been completed, we were freed.

XXVI. THIRD CONJUGATION. PRESENT STEM.

An Invitation to a Country-house refused.

1. While your letter is being read, I am oppressed with great envy.
2. I am surrounded with many labours; yet nothing is being done.
3. I shall be kept in the city for a long time; in vain am I drawn away by you.
4. While the republic shall be ruled by bad leaders, nothing will be done.
5. In vain will a happy life at your country-house be held-out.
6. We are overwhelmed with great burdens: we are bothered with many cares.
7. Many friendships are being formed (joined), nor however will the old-ones be neglected.
8. We shall ever rejoice, if we shall still be esteemed by you.
9. Very great thanks will be given to you for your great kindness.
10. While these words are being written, the letter-carrier has entered. Farewell.

XXVII. DEFINITIVE PRONOUNS. **IDEM**, 'Same.' **IPSE**, 'Self.'

Tribute to a Friend.

1. The same house belonged (was) to us, the same friends.
2. The same things were pleasing and the same things disagreeable to us.
3. He himself was in the number of those whom nature herself loads with honours.
4. We were always fond of the same things: never did I offend him in the smallest matter.
5. He himself often praised his friends, never did he blame the same.
6. He also (*idem*) used to load us with many rewards; he himself was content with few things.
7. If it is the mark of friends (*gen.*) to praise the same-things and blame the same-things, ours was true friendship.
8. At the same time he himself was always patient and humble.
9. The image of that same man will always be kept in-memory by me myself.
10. For the memory of the things themselves is not destroyed with the man himself.

XXVIII. THIRD CONJUGATION. PERFECT STEM.

Marius defeats the Teutons.

1. When these things had been carried out, war was declared.
2. The armies of the Teutons were led into Italy.
3. Immediately the Romans were conquered in three battles.

4. All in the city were oppressed with great fear.
5. Then Marius was elected general and sent to the army.
6. The war was carried on for three years, nor were the enemy conquered.
7. At last the barbarian forces were led out of camp.
8. The enemy were overthrown and crushed with great slaughter.
9. Marius, the conqueror of the barbarians, was cherished with great love.
10. And so the matter was well carried out: at last an end was put to the war.

XXIX. PRONOMINAL ADJECTIVES.

ALTER, 'ONE OF TWO'; 'THE ONE,' 'THE OTHER.'
ALIUS, 'ONE,' 'ANOTHER'; *in plur.*, 'SOME,' 'OTHERS.'

Caesar and Pompey.

1. To some citizens Caesar's cause was pleasing, to others Pompey's.
2. The senators had sent one general into Gaul, the other they kept in Italy.
3. The plan of one general was bad, the other was waiting an opportunity.
4. The senators desired one thing, the citizens another.
5. At this time some things were adverse to Caesar, some were favourable.
6. But when Caesar entered the city, Pompey with some citizens sailed to Greece; many others joined themselves to Caesar.
7. Caesar had led some legions to the city, others were hastening from Gaul.

8. In the Pharsalian battle fortune was kind to one leader, the other leader was overcome.

9. Out of Pompey's soldiers many were killed, others sailed with him to Egypt, others hastened to Italy.

10. It is one thing to start a war, another thing to gain the victory.

XXX. FOURTH CONJUNCTION. INDICATIVE MOOD.

PRESENT STEM.

A Letter from a Roman in Britain. B. C. 54.

1. During these six months we are hindered by many cares in Gaul.

2. While our ships are being got ready, many things are heard, nothing certain is known about the Britons.

3. Our course was often hindered by adverse winds and tides.

4. At last all things were being finished: then our course is directed to the island.

5. The shouts of the barbarians are heard far off on the sea.

6. The approaches of the island were being fortified: the harbours were being guarded.

7. Our men are not hindered by the barbarians; a way is soon opened up through the waves.

8. Nothing is known about the nature of the island: the inhabitants are clothed with skins against (*contra*) the cold.

9. If nothing shall be heard from (*ex*) you, you shall be punished.

10. My anger will only be calmed and appeased by many letters.

XXXI. FOURTH CONJUGATION. PERFECT STEM.

Defeat of Cassivellaunus, a British Chief.

1. Caesar's words were then heard by all the soldiers.
2. 'The camp of Cassivellaunus has been fortified by nature and by art.'
3. 'But you have never been hindered by danger from great deeds.'
4. 'If only a way shall have been opened up, you will not be stopped by fear of the enemy.'
5. 'The noise of your approach has not been heard by the barbarians.'
6. 'When they shall have been roused from sleep, they will be heavily punished.'
7. 'Our course has been hindered by woods and by marshes.'
8. 'Now you have been freed from all delay; soon your work will be finished by victory.'
9. At the same time his words were finished: at the same time a shout was heard.
10. The barbarians, by whom the camp had been guarded, were already in flight.

XXXII. DEMONSTRATIVE, INTERROGATIVE AND RELATIVE PRONOUNS.

A Visit to a Roman House.

Augustus. What shall we visit to-day? Have I not seen nearly everything which is worthy of mention?

Claudius. We will visit a splendid house, about which I have related much (*n. pl.*) to you. One of my friends is guarding it, while his master is absent.

Augustus. That which you advise is most suitable.

Claudius. 'Here-is the door! Knock! Beware of the dog!

Augustus. "With what care has the figure been painted !

Guardian. Who is there? What do you wish?

Claudius. It is I.   Good-day!

Guardian. For what reason do you hasten hither?

Claudius.   My friend, who is a stranger in the city, will give you thanks, if you shall have shown him the beautiful pictures and statues in this house.

Guardian. Nothing can be more pleasant to me than this.

XXXIII.   THE PRONOUNS.

A Visit to a Roman House (continued).

Guardian. Enter.   This is the hall.

Augustus. How beautiful is the marble floor of this hall !

Guardian. First we enter the large atrium.   Look at these pictures, at those marble statues !

Augustus. What is the story of that picture?

Guardian. Diogenes is saying to Alexander: 'A little away from the sun !'

Augustus. I have seen nothing more splendid than this court.   What beautiful columns !

Guardian. Look at these book-cases, which are filled with the writings of the best authors.

Augustus. Who is that first author, whose bust surpasses all the others?

Guardian. That is Socrates, who is saying: 'Why am I, who wrote nothing, placed here ?'

Augustus. What says his friend on the right?

Guardian. Plato advises him with these words: 'What have I written, except that which you said ?'

XXXIV. IRREGULAR VERBS.

VOLO, NŎLO, MĀLO.

Inauguration of the Australian Commonwealth. A. D. 1901.

Briton 1. I was wishing to see you. Lo! you are here!

Briton 2. Why were you willing to trust yourself to fortune? Why did you not prefer to send a letter?

Briton 1. He, to whom I had wished to give the letter, was unwilling to come hither.

Briton 2. But what do you wish to say to me?

Briton 1. Listen to that which I wished to write. We wish to visit Australia. If you shall be able and shall be willing, will you not sail with us?

Briton 2. I have always preferred to sail with you than with others. Now I shall prefer in vain.

Briton 1. If you wish to see Australia, and prefer to sail with me, why are you unwilling to come?

Briton 2. This year we shall be unwilling to undertake so long a journey.

Briton 1. But this year the commencement of the republic is being celebrated in Australia.

Briton 2. You advise well. If my wife shall be willing, I shall not be unwilling. Farewell!

XXXV. THE VERB ĪRE, 'To go,' and its Compounds.

A Journey from Brundisium to Rome.

Marcus. Whence do you return to Rome? All at home were grieving because you were absent.

Quintus. I have returned from Baiae. I left the ship to-day.

Marcus. I am glad that (because) you have returned home. Did you not see Horatius at Baiae?

Quintus. He had gone to Puteoli before (*conj.*) I reached Baiae. Afterwards I saw him at Puteoli.

Marcus. When will Horatius return to Rome?

Quintus. He will never depart from Baiae, unless he shall have departed from (*e*) life.

Marcus. Why does he live at Baiae?

Quintus. He is kept there by the Lucrine oysters. He never goes out of his villa.

Marcus. Surely your brother lives at Naples? Did you not go to Naples and Pompeii?

Quintus. At Cumae I went on board a ship and sailed to Naples, but my brother had just gone away to Pompeii.

XXXVI.

A Journey from Brundisium to Rome (*continued*).

Marcus. Whither did you go then?

Quintus. I remained three days at Naples at my brother's house. On the third day the letter-carrier returned from Pompeii.

Marcus. But what had your brother written?

Quintus. He had given no letters to the letter-carrier. Then we got ready our horses and hastened our journey to Pompeii.

Marcus. It is a most pleasant place. How many days were you at Pompeii?

Quintus. Scarcely had we gone forth from Naples, when my brother met us.

Marcus. You did not (*num*) return to Naples, whence you had just departed?

Quintus. My brother was returning home but wished at once to go to Puteoli.

Marcus. I am always sorry that I have never been at Puteoli.

Quintus. It is a crowded place. Many approach from all sides to Puteoli to the mineral-waters.

Marcus. Farewell! It is necessary to go home. While I was working at Rome, you were surrounded in-the-country by all sorts of pleasures.

XXXVII. VERBS IN -IO. THIRD CONJUGATION.

The Carthaginians invade Italy.

1. The republic was in great danger; all the citizens take up arms.
2. Many disasters were being received: the State was being visited with severe wounds.
3. At last the consul makes an attack upon (*in*) the Carthaginians.
4. Many Romans are being killed: more are being captured in flight.
5. In vain the generals address (make) words to the soldiers.
6. 'It will be better if we shall be killed than if we shall flee.'
7. 'If you shall fail in-courage, a heavy disaster will be received.'
8. No one does what the generals desire: the soldiers, blind with fear, flee in all directions.
9. Many weapons were being thrown by the enemy: many Romans were being killed.
10. Night makes an end of the flight: the tired Carthaginians betake themselves to camp.

XXXVIII. DEPONENT VERBS.

Death of Queen Victoria, Jan. 22nd, 1901.

1. How shall we speak about the death of our queen ?
   With what words shall we recall her life ?
2. Hope consoles the wretched : her illustrious example
   will always console and exhort us.
3. She has died full of years, full of honour, full of
   the love of her citizens.
4. If we shall contemplate her life, we shall admire
   her goodness and wisdom.
5. She shared her joys and sorrows with (*cum*) her
   citizens : she strove for her country, not for
   herself.
6. Nor do we in Britain alone suffer this sorrow.
7. The citizens of our colonies and of the whole world
   revered our queen and suffer the same grief.
8. And now the son of our king sets out for the shores
   of the great colonies.
9. The citizens will honour this prince on account of
   the memory of the queen.
10. I have attempted a difficult task, but I shall not
    fear this : I shall not seem worthy of blame,
    if I shall have spoken ill.

RECAPITULATORY

XXXIX.

Cyclops complains to his father Neptune about Ulysses.

Cyclops. O father, have you not heard my cries ? I have
suffered a great injury.

Neptune. Who has attempted to wrong my son?

Cyclops. A stranger, who came to the shores of my island, has blinded me.

Neptune. But how was he able to do this?

Cyclops. Not by courage, but by cunning was I overcome.

Neptune. What mortal surpasses my son in-cunning?

Cyclops. He himself said to me: 'Nobody is my (*mihi*) name.' But afterwards he was called Ulysses by his companions.

Neptune. How was my son deceived by these foolish words? Where did the stranger attack you?

Cyclops. I had just led back my sheep to the cave. The door had been closed with the immense rock and a fire had been lighted in the cave. Then I saw 'Nobody' and his companions among the sheep. Soon he gave me sweet wine and I was overcome by sleep.

XL.

Complaint of Cyclops (*continued*).

Neptune. But while your eye was being blinded (*pres. tense*), were you not awakened from sleep?

Cyclops. I was awakened and cried out, 'Nobody is attacking me.' And so my companions came not to my aid (*dat.*). Thus I was overcome by the cunning of the stranger.

Neptune. But how did Ulysses escape out of the cave? Was he (*num*) able to move the stone from the entrance?

Cyclops. I myself had moved the stone and was waiting for 'Nobody' on the threshold of the cave.

Neptune. Of course he was concealed among the s
and was not seen by you.

Cyclops. What shall I do? How shall I punish
wicked Greek?

Neptune. While he is sailing on my ocean, he shall
a worthy penalty to me. Not without injury shall
return home.

VOCABULARIES

N. B.—*Only long syllables have the quantities marked.*

I.

auctumnus, -i, 2 *m.*, autumn.

auris, -is, 3 *f.*, an ear.

creo, 1 *v. a.*, I create.

Grātiae, -ārum, 1 *f. pl.*, the Graces (goddesses of beauty).

Olympias, -adis, 3 *f.*, an Olympiad (space of four years between the celebration of the games at Olympia).

Olympius, -a, -um, *adj.*, Olympian (of Olympia, a town in the West of Greece).

operārius, -a, -um, *adj.*, working.

sensus, -ūs, 4 *m.*, sense.

spatium, -ii, 2 *n.*, space.

vel, *conj.*, or (aut excludes one thing; vel gives the choice of either).

vēr, vēris, 3 *n.*, spring (of the year).

II.

aedificium, -ii, 2 *n.*, a building.

Biās,-antis, 3 *m.*, Bias (a Cretan).

cremo, 1 *v. a.*, I burn.

dīvido, -vīsi, -vīsum, 3 *v. a.*, I divide.

initium, -ii, 2 *n.*, beginning.

maximē, *adv.*, most, especially.

mensis, -is, 3 *m.*, a month.

mirāculum, -i, 2 *n.*, a wonder, marvel.

pretium, -ii, 2 *n.*, price.

Sibyllinus, -a, -um, *adj.*, of the Sibyl, Sibylline (the Sibyls were prophetic women).

Sōlon, -ōnis, 3 *m.*, Solon (a famous Athenian).

Thalēs, -is, 3 *m.*, Thales (a philosopher).

vetulus, -a, -um, *adj.*, old.

III.

Albāni, -ōrum, 2 *m. pl.*, the Albans (inhabitants of Alba Longa, a city near Rome).

Ětrūria, -ae, 1 *f.*, Etruria (a country north of Rome).

imperātor, -ōris, 3 *m.*, an emperor.

Latīni,-ōrum, 2 *m.pl.*, the Latins (inhabitants of Latium, in which country Rome was situated).

Sabīni, -ōrum, 2 *m. pl.*, the Sabines (neighbours of the Latins).

speciēs, -ēi, 5 *f.*, form, shape.

IV.

Aegyptius, -a, -um, *adj.*, Egyptian.

Artemisia, -ae, 1 *f.*, Artemisia.

Cāria,-ae, 1 *f.*, Caria (a province of Asia Minor).

Ephesius, -a, -um, *adj.*, of Ephesus.

lātus, -a, -um, *adj.*, broad.

marītus, -i, 2 *m.*, husband.

Mausōlus, -i, 2 *m.*, Mausolus (king of Caria).

Nīlus, -i, 2 *m.*, the Nile.

sepulcrum, -i, 2 *n.*, tomb.

V.

Alexandrīnus, -a, -um, *adj.*, of Alexandria.

Cannensis, -e, *adj.*, of Cannae.

columna, -ae, 1 *f.*, a pillar, column.

Marathōnius, -a, -um, *adj.*, of Marathon.

modo, *adv.*, only.

passus, -ūs, 4 *m.*, a pace.

pendeo,pependi,pensum, 2*v.n.*, I hang, am suspended.

Persicus, -a, -um, *adj.*, Persian.

Pharus, -i, 2 *f.*, a lighthouse (on the island of Pharos).

Plataeae,-ārum, 1 *f. pl.*,Plataea.

signum, -i, 2 *n.*, a statue.

supersum, *v. n.*, I survive.

VI.

certo, 1 *v. a.*, I decide by contest, contend.

consulto, 1 *v. a.*, I consult, deliberate.

contendo, -di, -tum, 3 *v. n.*, I contend, try my strength.

curro, cucurri, cursum, 3 *v. n.*, I run.

cursus, -ūs, 4 *m.*, running.

frau3, fraudis, 3 *f.*, a trick.

lūsus, -ūs, 4 *m.*, a game.

necesse, *indecl. neut. adj.*, necessary.

possum, posse, potui, *v. n.*, I am able.

sententia, -ae, 1 *f.*, an opinion.

saltus, -ūs, 4 *m.*, jumping, leaping.

stadium, -ii, 2 *n.*, a racecourse.

studeo, 2 *v. n.*, I desire, am anxious.

VII.

consūmo, -sumpsi, -sumptum, 3 v.a., I waste.

erro, 1 v. n., I wander from the truth, err.

hūmānus, -a, -um, adj., natural to man, human.

pecco, 1 v. n., I sin.

ūtilis, -e, adj., useful.

VIII.

amābilis, -e, adj., worthy of love, amiable.

amplus, -a, -um, adj., great, ample.

coniunctus, -a, -um, adj., close, intimate.

fingo, finxi, fictum, 3 v. a., I invent, devise.

firmus, -a, -um, adj., firm.

gravis, -e, adj., heavy.

integritas, -ātis, 3 f., integrity.

iūs, iūris, 3 n., law.

levis, -e, adj., light.

nihil, n. indecl., nothing.

opulentus, -a, -um, adj., rich.

praestans, -antis, adj., remarkable, excellent.

reddo, reddidi, redditum, 3 v. a., I render.

splendidus, -a, -um, adj., brilliant, splendid.

studiōsus, -a, -um, adj., eager (with gen.).

unquam, adv., ever.

IX.

accumbo, -cubui, -cubitum, 3 v. n., I recline at table.

ātrium, -i, 2 n., the hall or chief room of a house.

caveo, cāvi, cautum, 2 v. n. and a., I take care.

cursus, -ūs, 4 m., a course.

dēligo, -lēgi, -lectum, 3 v. a., I choose.

dēmo, dempsi, demptum, 3 v. a., I take away.

heus, interj., ho there! holloa!

hilaris, -e, adj., merry.

infrā, adv., below.

lavo, 1 v. a., I wash.

libet, 2 v. impers., it pleases.

ministro, 1 v. a., I wait upon, hand, serve.

monstro, 1 v. a., I show.

paulisper, adv., for a little time.

prior, comp. adj., former, first.

pulso, 1 v. a., I knock at.

rectus, -a, -um, adj., straight.

removeo, -mōvi, -mōtum, 2 v. a, I remove.

solea, -ae, 1 f., a sandal (worn in the house only).

taceo, 2 v. n., I am silent.

triclīnium, -i, 2 n., a couch (round three sides of a dining-table); hence a dining-room.

X.

anas, anatis, 3 *f.*, a duck.

appŏno, -posui, -positum, 3 *v. a.*, I set before, serve up.

bibo, *perf.* bibi, 3 *v. a.*, I drink.

castanea, -ae, 1 *f.*, chestnut.

dīmidius, -a, -um, *adj.*, half.

discerpo, -cerpsi, -cerptum, 3 *v. a.*, I cut in pieces, carve.

fundo, fūdi, fūsum, 3 *v. a.*, I pour out.

gallīna, -ae, 1 *f.*, a hen, fowl.

impleo, -āvi, -ētum, 2 *v. a.*, I fill up.

lacerna, -ae, 1 *f.*, a cloak.

lego, lēgi, lectum, 3 *v. a.*, I read.

mensa, -ae, 1 *f.*, a table; secunda mensa, dessert, (when both dishes and table were changed).

misceo, miscui, mixtum, 2 *v. a.*, I mix.

mūraena, -ae, 1 *f.*, an eel (found in the sea).

ostrea, -ae, 1 *f.*, an oyster.

pănis, -is, 3 *m.*, bread.

pōculum, -i, 2 *n.*, a goblet.

pŏmum, -i, 2 *n.*, fruit, apple.

prōmissum, -i, 2 *n.*, a promise.

rĕpleo, -ēvi, -ētum, 2 *v. a.*, I fill again.

scindo, scidi, scissum, 3 *v. a.*, I cut, carve.

titulus, -i, 2 *m.*, an inscription.

tollo, sustuli, sublātum, 3 *v. a.*, I take away

XI.

Alexander, -dri, 2 *m.*, Alexander.

aurum, -i, 2 *n.*, gold.

Babylōn, -ōnis, 3 *f.*, Babylon (chief city of Babylonia on the Euphrates).

cūro, 1 *v. a.*, I look after, take care of.

eŏ, *adv.*, so much, by so much (with *comparative*).

fortasse, *adv.*, perhaps.

Macedones, -um, 3 *m. plur.*, the Macedonians.

pondus, -eris, 3 *n.*, weight.

puto, 1 *v. a.*, I think (with *double accusative*).

quō, *adv.*, by how much (with *comparative*).

spĕro, 1 *v. a.*, I hope.

XII.

ā, ab, *prep.*, by (*with ablative of the person only*).

adeo, *adv.*, so, so much.

concilium, -i, 2 *n.*, a council, gathering.

convoco, 1 *v. a.*, I call together.

crucio, 1 *v. a.*, I torture.

ignāvia, -ae, 1 *f.*, cowardice.

incommodum, -i, 2 *n.*, disaster.

perturbo, 1 *v. a.*, I disturb.

posterus, -a, -um, *adj.*, next.

sollicito, 1 *v. a.*, I distress.

vītupero, 1 *v. a.*, I blame, censure.

XIII.

argentum, -i, 2 *n.*, silver, money.

exemplum, -i, 2 *n.*, an example.

explōro, 1 *v. a.*, I examine.

frūgālitas, -ātis, 3 *f.*, frugality.

luxuria, -ae, 1 *f.*, luxury.

luxuriōsus, -a, -um, *adj.*, extravagant, luxurious.

paupertas, -ātis, 3 *f.*, poverty.

potestas, -ātis, 3 *f.*, power.

rusticus, -a, -um, *adj.*, rustic, rural.

XIV.

dēsum, *v. n.*, I fail, am wanting (*dat. of pers.*).

dubius, -a, -um, *adj.*, doubtful.

exitium, -i, 2 *n.*, destruction.

fēlīcitas, -ātis, 3 *f.*, good luck, fortune, happiness.

fēlīciter, *adv.*, luckily.

impedīmentum, -i, 2 *n.*, a hindrance.

instruo, 3 *v. a.*, I draw up.

is, ea, id, *pron.*, that; he, she, it.

nuntio, 1 *v. a.*, I announce, report.

perpetuus, -a, -um, *adj.*, everlasting, unfailing.

ubǐ, *adv.*, when.

undique, *adv.*, from all sides.

XV.

Aequi, -ōrum, 2 *m. pl.*, the Aequians (a warlike people near Rome).

arātrum, -i, 2 *n.*, a plough.

consīdero, 1 *v. a.*, I examine.

dictātūra, -ae, 1 *f.*, dictatorship.

mūnus, -eris, 3 *n.*, a gift, present.

rectē, *adv.*, rightly.

rusticus, -a, -um, *adj.*, rustic, rural.

Samnītes, -ium, 3 *m. pl.*, the Samnites (a tribe south of Rome).

sollicito, 1 *v. a.*, I tempt.

tento, 1 *v. a.*, I try, tamper with.

XVI.

auctōritas, -ātis, 3 *f.*, authority.

avāritia, -ae, 1 *f.*, avarice.

cīvīlis, -e, *adj.*, civil.

divitiae, -ārum, 1 *f. pl.*, riches.

firmitas, -ātis, 3 *f.*, strength.

grātīs, *adv.*, free, without payment.

gravitas, -ātis, 3 *f.*, weight, importance.

honestas, -ātis, 3 *f.*, honesty.

id temporis, at that time.

magistrātus, -ūs, 4 *m.*, a magistrate.

nimis, *adv.*, too much.

parum, *adv.*, little, too little.

pătres, -um, 3 *m.*, the senators.

penes, *prep. with acc.*, in the hands of, in the power of.

H 2

XVII

comparo, 1 *v. a.*, I compare (*with prep.* cum).

dēfatīgo, 1 *v. a.*, I exhaust, tire.

exanimo, 1 *v. a.*, I alarm or deprive of courage.

lătro, -ōnis, 3 *m.*, a robber.

Leōnidas, -ae, 1 *m.*, Leonidas (*Voc.* Leōnida).

Mīnos, -ōis, 3 *m.*, Minos (a judge in the lower world).

nu:n, *an interrogative* ɪ *expecting a negative a*

prŏbrum, -i, 2 *n.*, abuse, ɪ

satelles, -itis, 3 *m.*, an a ant (on a distingɪ person).

valdē, *adv.*, greatly, e: ingly.

vexo, 1 *v. a.*, I harass, aɪ

XVIII.

Cynicus, -i, 2 *m.*, a Cynic philosopher, a Cynic (from the Greek 'dog-like').

dēdecus, -oris, 3 *n.*, a disgrace.

Diogenes, -is, 3 *m.*, Diogenes (the Cynic philosopher).

Epicūrus, -i, 2 *m.*, Epicurus (the famous philosopher who held pleasure to be the highest good).

iuventūs, -ūtis, 3 *f.*, youtl

longē, *adv.*, far.

mollitia, -ae, 1 *f.*, softnes:

paululum, *adv.*, a little.

pōno, posui, positum, 3 ɪ I place, reckon.

sīcărius, -i, 2 *m.*, an assas:

termino, 1 *v. a.*, I limit, de

Zēno, -ōnis, 3 *m.*, Zeno (fou of the Stoic philosopl

XIX.

augeo, auxi, auctum, 2 *v. a.*, I increase.

dēfleo, -ēvi, -ētum, 2 *v. a.*, I lament, weep over.

dēterreo, 2 *v. a.*, I frighten from (*prep.* dē *with abl.*).

factum, -i, 2 *n.*, a deed.

fāma, -ae, 1 *f.*, fame, renown.

furor -ōris, 3 *m.*, madness.

ingrātus, -a, -um, *adj.*, grateful.

laus, laudis, 3 *f.*, praise.

nempe, *adv.*, certainly, w out doubt.

obsideo, -sēdi, -sessum, 2 *v.* I besiege, attack.

societas, -ātis, 3 *f.*, fellowsl association.

vānus, -a, -um, *adj.*, useles:

XX.

aequus, -a, -um, *adj.*, fair, equal.

condicio, -ōnis, 3 *f.*, condition, terms.

foedus, -eris, 3 *n.*, a treaty.

nātio, -ōnis, 3 *f.*, a tribe.

opus est, it is needful, wanting (*with dat. of person, abl. of thing wanted*).

orbis, -is, 3 *m.*, a circle ; hence orbis terrarum, the circle of the earth, the world.

regio, -ōnis, 3 *f.*, a region, district.

satio, 1 *v. a.*, I satisfy.

sitis, -is, 3 *f.*, thirst (*acc.* sitim, *abl.* siti).

XXI.

dēlectus, -ūs, 4 *m.*, a levy (of troops).

habeo, 2 *v. a.*, I have, hold, consider ; habeo fidem,

I place confidence (*with dat. of person*).

retineo, retinui, retentum, 2 *v. a.*, I hold back.

XXII.

colloco, 1 *v. a.*, I settle.

commoveo, -mōvi, -mōtum, 2 *v. a.*, I bring about, raise.

destituo, -ui, -ūtum, 3 *v. a.*, I forsake, desert.

fīnis, -is, 3 *m.*, end.

graviter, *adv.*, heavily, severely.

imperitus, -a, -um, *adj.*, unskilled.

impōno, -posui, -positum, 3 *v. a.*, I place, put (*with indirect dat.*).

maritimus, -a, -um, *adj.*, of the sea, maritime.

plūrimum, *super. adv.*, very, very much.

prior, -us, *comp. adj.*, former, previous.

propitius, -a, -um, *adj.*, favourable, propitious.

sto, steti, statum, 1 *v. n.*, I stand.

superior, -us, *comp. adj.*, superior, stronger.

XXIII.

Alpes, -ium, 3 *f.*, the Alps.
crūdēliter, *adv.*, cruelly.
deinde, *adv.*, then, thereupon.
Hispānia, -ae, 1 *f.*, Spain.
impetro, 1 *v. a.*, I obtain (by asking).

Saguntum, -i, 2 *n.*, Sagu
supplicium, -i, 2 *n.*, pʊ
    ment, torture.
ūtilis, -e, *adj.*, useful, eƷ
    ent.

XXIV.

aequo, 1 *v. a.*, I make one thing equal to another, I level (*with acc. and dat.*).
avus, -i, 2 *m.*, a grandfather.
cognōmen, -inis, 3 *n.*, a surname, family name.
decus, -oris, 3 *n.*, an ornament.
mitto, mīsi, missum, 3 *v. a.*, I send.
pār, paris, *adj.*, equal to, a match for (*with dat.*).

pax, pācis, 3 *f.*, peace.
prōfligo, 1 *v. a.*, I overth
    utterly defeat.
renovo, 1 *v. a.*, I renew.
revoco, 1 *v. a.*, I recall.
Scīpio, -ōnis, 3 *m.*, Scipio.
solum, -i, 2 *n.*, the groun⊂
triumphus, -i, 2 *m.*, a triuɪ
    (triumphum ago, I ⊂
    braṭe a triumph).

XXV.

ēmendo, 1 *v. a.*, I free from faults, improve.
explico, 1 *v. a.*, I explain.
ferula, -ae, 1 *f.*, a whip, rod.
fides, -ium, 3 *f. plur.*, a stringed instrument, lyre.
Horātius, -i, 2 *m.*, Horace.
importo, 1 *v. a.*, I bring in, introduce.
instituo, -ui, -ūtum, 3 *v. a.*, I train, instruct.
litterārius, -a, -um, *adj.*, of or belonging to reading and writing; *hence* lūdus litterārius, an elementary school.

māne, *n. indecl.*, in the morni
mūsicus, -a, -um, *adj.*, musi⊂
    hence mūsica, -ōrᵾ
    2 *n. pl.*, music.
paedagōgus, -i, 2 *m.*, a ⱷ
    ceptor (slave who looᴋ
    after children and tɕ
    them to school).
palaestra, -ae, 1 *f.*, wrestlⁱ
    school (for young boys'
retracto, 1 *v. a.*, I han⊂
    again, revise.
Vergilius, -i, 2 *m.*, Vergil.
versor, -ātus, 1 *pass.*, I a
    engaged.

XXVI.

abstraho, -xi, -ctum, 3 *v. a.*, I draw away.

addūco, -xi, -ctum, 3 *v. a.*, I lead to, induce.

ango, -xi, -ctum, 3 *v. a.*, I pain, bother.

dēfendo, -di, -sum, 3 *v. a.*, I defend.

fundus, -i, 2 *m.*, a farm.

interpōno, -posui, -positum, 3 *v. a.*, I let pass, leave (an interval).

ostendo, -di, -sum *and* -tum, 3 *v. a.*, I show, hold out.

premo, pressi, pressum, 3 *v. a.*, I press, overwhelm, oppress.

sollicitūdo, -inis, 3 *f.*, care, anxiety.

tabellārius, -i, 2 *m.*, a letter-carrier.

veho, vexi, vectum, I carry; *in pass.*, I am carried, ride.

XXVII.

domus, -ūs, 2 *and* 4 *f.*, a house (*abl. sing.* domo, *acc. plur.* domos; *other cases like* 4 *decl.*).

imāgo, -inis, 3 *f.*, an image.

invītus, -a, -um, *adj.*, unwilling.

offendo, -di, -sum, 3 *v. a.*, I offend.

sentio, sensi, sensum, 4 *v. a.*, I feel.

victus, -ūs, 4 *m.*, way of living.

voluntas, -ātis, 3 *f.*, wish.

vultus, -ūs, 4 *m.*, face, countenance.

XXVIII.

adfligo, -ixi, -ictum, 3 *v. a.*, I cast down, overthrow.

destruo, -xi, -ctum, 3 *v. a.*, I destroy.

ēligo, -ēgi, -ectum, 3 *v. a.*, I elect.

exstinguo, -nxi, -nctum, 3 *v. a.*, I destroy, annihilate.

opprimo, -essi, -essum, 3 *v. a.*, I crush, overwhelm.

perdūco, -xi, -ctum, 3 *v. a.*, I lead through, bring.

tergum, -i, 2 *n.*, back, rear.

Teutoni, -ōrum, 2 *m. pl.*, the Teutons (German tribe).

trādo, -didi, -ditum, 3 *v. a.*, I hand over.

XXIX.

adiuvo, -iūvi, -iūtum, 1 v. a., I assist, support.

Aegyptus, -i, 2 f., Egypt.

cēdo, cessi, cessum, 3 v. a., I yield.

cupīdo, -inis, 3 f., desire.

dīvitiae, -ārum, 1 f. pl., wealth, riches.

factio, -ōnis, 3 f., a party, faction.

glōria, -ae, 1 f., glory.

occāsio, -ōnis, 3 f., opportunity.

Pharsālius, -a, -um, adj., of Pharsalus, Pharsalian.

Pharsālus, -i, 2 f., Pharsalus (a city in Thessaly).

trucīdo, 1 v. a., I slaughter, kill.

XXX.

caro, carnis, 3 f., flesh.

certus, -a, -um, adj., certain.

frūmentum, -i, 2 n., corn.

incursio, -ōnis, 3 f., an attack.

lac, lactis, 3 n., milk.

lāna, -ae, 1 f., wool.

lēnio, 4 v. a., I calm, appease.

līnum, -i, 2 n., linen.

mōles, -is, 3 f., a huge structure, a pier, mole.

nisi, conj., if not, unless.

reperio, repperi, repertum, 4 v. a., I find, discover.

XXXI.

agmen, -inis, 3 n., a column, army (on the march).

Cassivellaunus, -i, 2 m., Cassivellaunus.

excio, 4 v. a., I rouse.

līberi, -ōrum, 2 m. pl., children.

magnopere, adv., greatly.

palūs, -ūdis, 3 f., a marsh.

simul, adv., at the same time, at once.

strepitus, -ūs, 4 m., noise, din.

XXXII.

libenter, adv., gladly, willingly.

mendīcus, -i, 2 m., a beggar.

pingo, pinxi, pictum, 3 v. a., I paint.

vestibulum, -i, 2 n., an entrance-hall, entrance.

vīso, vīsi, vīsum, 3 v. a., I visit.

XXXIII.

cubiculum, -i, 2 *n.*, a bedroom.

fauces, -ium, 3 *f.*, corridor, passage.

imāgo, -inis, 3 *f.*, bust, statue.

impluvium, -i, 2 *n.*, a square basin in the atrium, into which the rain fell, through an opening in the roof.

peristȳlium, -i, 2 *n.*, a court (the centre space being open and surrounded by columns).

piscīna, -ae, 1 *f.*, a fountain, basin (in which fish were often kept).

pluteus, -i, 2 *m.*, a book-case (on which busts of the authors were also placed).

postīcum, -i, 2 *n.*, a back-door.

prŏprius, -a, -um, *adj.*, not common with others, private.

sŏlum, -i, 2 *n.*, the ground; *hence*, the floor or pavement.

spectāculum, -i, 2 *n.*, a show, spectacle.

tabulīnum, -i, 2 *n.*, an office, writing-room (*from* tabella, writing-tablet).

XXXIV.

Austrālia, -ae, 1 *f.*, Australia (the southern land).

Canada, -ae, 1 *f.*, Canada.

committo, -mīsi, -missum, 3 *v. a.*, I trust, entrust.

regio, -ōnis, 3 *f.*, district, country.

sērius, -a, -um, *adj.*, serious.

vir, viri, 2 *m.*, a husband.

XXXV.

abeo, -īre, -ii, -itum, *v. n.*, I go away, leave, depart.

abhinc, *adv.*, ago, since.

adeo, -īre, -ii, -itum, *v. n.*, I go to, approach.

Brundisium, -i, 2 *n.*, Brindisi.

conscendo, -di, -sum, 3 *v. a.*, I embark, go on board (*prep.* in *and acc.*).

exeo, -īre, -ii, -itum, *v. n.*, I go out, depart, leave (*prep.* ex *or* de).

illūc, *adv.*, thither.

ineo, -īre, -ii, -itum, *v. n.*, I go in, enter upon, enter.

modo, *adv.*, just.

Neāpolis, -is, 3 *f.*, Naples (*acc.* -im, *abl.* -i).

prōdeo, -īre, -ii, -itum, *v. n.*, I go *or* come forth.

Puteoli, -ōrum, 2 *m. pl.*, Puteoli (near Naples).

redeo, -īre, -ii, -itum, *v. n.*, I return.

rūs, rūris, 3 *n.*, the country (*opp.* town).

tranquillus, -a, -um, *adj.*, quiet, peaceful.

turbulentus, -a, -um, *adj.*, noisy.

XXXVI.

aquae, -ārum, 1 *f. pl.*, mineral waters, springs.

āter, -tra, -trum, *adj.*, black.

Beneventum, -i, 2 *n.*, Beneventum.

Capua, -ae, 1 *f.*, Capua.

caupo, -ōnis, 3 *m.*, landlord.

imber, -bris, 3 *m.*, rain.

incendium, -i, 2 *n.*, a house on fire, conflagration, blaze.

incendo, -di, -sum, 3 *v. a.*, I set on fire.

iocōsus, -a, -um, *adj.*, witty.

obviam, *adv.*, in the way; *with* eo, I go to meet, I meet (*with dat. of person*).

pānis, -is, 3 *m.*, bread.

sevērus, -a, -um, *adj.*, serious, severe, stern.

unā, *adv.*, in company, together.

XXXVII.

capio, cēpi, captum, 3 *v. a.*, I take, capture; accipio, I receive; recipio, I betake.

cupio, cupīvi, cupītum, 3 *v. a.*, I desire.

facio, fēci, factum, 3 *v. a.*, I make; verba facio, I speak, plead; afficio, I visit with, afflict; dēficio, I fail; interficio, I kill.

fugio, fūgi, fugitum, 3 *v. n.*, I flee, escape.

iacio, iēci, iactum, 3 *v. a.*, I throw; dēicio, I cast down; trāicio, I cross.

impetus, -ūs, 4 *m.*, an attack.

rapio, rapui, raptum, 3 *v. a.*, I seize, carry off.

undique, *adv.*, on all sides.

NOTE.—Compounds of **capio, facio** and **iacio** change a to i in the present stem, as **ac-cipio**: and a to e in the supine, as **ac-ceptum**.

XXXVIII.

admiror, 1 *v. dep.*, I admire.

aemulor, 1 *v. dep.*, I strive after, try to equal.

comitor, 1 *v. dep.*, I accompany.

cōnor, 1 *v. dep.*, I attempt.

consōlor, 1 *v. dep.*, I console.

contemplor, 1 *v. dep.*, I contemplate.

frustror, 1 *v. dep.*, I frustrate.

fūnus, -eris, 3 *n.*, death, funeral.

hortor, 1 *v. dep.*, I exhort.

imitor, 1 *v. dep.*, I imitate.

laetor, 1 *v. dep.*, I rejoice.

loquor, locūtus, 3 *v. dep.*, I speak.

mereor, 2 *v. dep.*, I deserve.

moderor, 1 *v. dep.*, I govern.

morior, mortuus, 3 *v. dep.*, I die.

nītor, nīsus, 3 *v. dep.*, I strive.

partior, 4 *v. dep.*, I share.

patior, passus, 3 *v. dep.*, I suffer.

preces, -um, 3 *f. plur.*, prayers.

princeps, -ipis, 3 *m.*, a prince.

probitas, -ātis, 3 *f.*, goodness.

proficiscor, profectus, 3 *v. dep.*, I set out.

quamquam, *conj.* although.

recordor, 1 *v. dep.*, I recall.

sequor, secūtus, 3 *v. dep.*, I follow.

templum, -i, 2 *n.*, a temple.

veneror, 1 *v. dep.*, I revere, honour.

vereor, 2 *v. dep.*, I fear.

videor, vīsus, 2 *v. dep.*, I seem.

XXXIX.

accendo, -di, -sum, 3 *v. a.*, I light, kindle.

adhibeo, 2 *v. a.*, I use, apply.

callidus, -a, -um, *adj.*, cunning.

certiorem facio, I inform, acquaint.

claudo, -si, -sum, 3 *v. a.*, I shut.

committo, -mīsi, -missum, 3 *v. a.*, I commit.

contemno, -tempsi, -temptum, 3 *v. a.*, I despise.

dēcipio, -cēpi, -ceptum, 3 *v. a.*, I deceive.

facinus, -oris, 3 *n.*, an outrage.

iniūria, -ae, 1 *f.*, an injury, wrong, loss.

pello, pepuli, pulsum, 3 *v. a.*, I drive.

pererro, 1 *v. a.*, I wander over.

redūco, 3 *v. a.*, I lead back.

violo, 1 *v. a.*, I outrage, wrong.

XL.

conspicio, -spexi, -spectum, 3
     v. a., I see, catch sight of.
dēsero, -serui, -sertum, 3 v. a.,
     I desert.
ēripio, -ripui, -reptum, 3 v. a.,
     I snatch away.

furor, -ōris, 3 m., rage.
responsum, -i, 2 n., an answ
ut, conj., as.

LATIN-ENGLISH INDEX

N.B.—*Only long syllables have the quantities marked.*

ă, ab, *prep. with abl.*, from, by.

ab-eo, -īre, -ii, itum, *v. n.*, I go away, depart.

abhinc, *adv.*, ago, since.

abs-traho, -ere, -xi, -ctum, 3 *v. a.*, I withdraw.

ab-sum, ab-esse, ă-fui, *v. n.*, I am absent, am distant.

ac-cendo, -ere, -ndi, -nsum, 3 *v. a.*, I kindle.

ac-cipio, -ere, -cēpi, -ceptum, 3 *v. a.*, I receive, accept.

ac-cumbo, -ere, -cubui, -cubitum, 3 *v. n.*, I recline at table.

ăcer, -cris, -cre, *adj.*, keen, fiery.

aciēs, -ēī, 5 *f.*, line-of-battle, army.

ad, *prep. with acc.*, (*of place*) to, toward, at; (*of time*) up to.

ad-dūco, -ere, -xi, -ctum, 3 *v. a.*, I lead toward, bring.

adeo, *adv.*, so, so much.

ad-eo, -īre, -ii, -itum, *v. n.*, I go to, approach.

ades, *pres. imperat. of* adsum, come !

ad-flīgo, -ere, -xi, -ctum, 3 *v. a.*, I cast down, overthrow.

ad-hibeo, -ēre, -ui, -itum, 2 *v. a.*, I use, employ.

adhūc, *adv.*, still, yet.

aditus, -ūs, 4 *m.*, approach, entrance.

ăd-iuvo, -āre, -iūvi, -iūtum, 1 *v. a.*, I help, assist, side with.

ad-ministro, 1 *v. a.*, I administer, manage.

ad-mīror, -āri, -ātus sum, 1 *v. dep.*, I admire.

ad-sum, -esse, -fui, *v. n.*, I am present, come, am here.

advena, -ae, 1 *m.*, a stranger.

adventus, -ūs, 4 *m.*, arrival.

adversus, -a, -um, *adj.*, adverse; adversae res, adversity.

aedificium, -i, 2 *n.*, a building.

aedifico, 1 *v. a.*, I build.

Aegyptius, -a, -um, *adj.*, Egyptian.

Aegyptus, -i, 2 *f.*, Egypt.

aemulor, -āri, -ātus sum, 1 *v. dep.*, I vie with, rival.

Aenēas, -ae, 1 *m.*, Aeneas.

aēneus, -a, -um, *adj.*, brazen.

Aequi, -ōrum, 2 *m. pl.*, the Aequians.

aequo, 1 *v. a.*, I make level; aequare solo, to level with the ground.

aequus, -a, -um, *adj.*, equal, fair.

aestas, -ātis, 3 *f.*, summer.

aestimo, 1 *v. a.*, I value; *with gen. of price*, plūris, more highly; minōris, at a smaller price, &c.

aestus, -ūs, 4 *m.*, tide.

Africa, -ae, 1 *f.*, Africa.

Africānus, -a, -um, *adj.*, African; a surname of Scipio.

ā-fui, *see* ab-sum.

ager, ăgri, 2 *m.*, field, land.

agmen, -inis, 3 *n.*, an army (on the march).

ago, -ere, ēgi, actum, 3 *v. a.*, I do, spend; ago causam, I take the side of; ago grātias, I give thanks; ago triumphum, I celebrate a triumph; ago rem, I discuss *or* deal with a matter.

ăgricola, -ae, 1 *m.*, a farmer.

āla, -ae, 1 *f.*, a wing.

Albāni, -ōrum, 2 *m. pl.*, the Albans.

Alexander, -dri, 2 *m.*, Alexander.

Alexandrīnus, -a, -um, *adj.*, of Alexandria.

alius, -a, -ud, *adj.*, one, other, another (of many); *repeated in another case*, one another, some . . . others.

Alpes, -ium, 3 *f.*, the Alps

alter, -era, -erum, *adj.*, other of two, one of t~ the other.

altus, -a, -um, *adj.*, high, ta

amābilis, -e, *adj.*, amiable.

amīcitia, -ae, 1 *f.*, friendshi

amīcus, -i, 2 *m.*, a friend.

amo, 1 *v. a.*, I love.

amor, -ōris, 3 *m.*, love.

amplus, -a, -um, *adj.*, ampl large.

anas, -atis, 3 *f.*, a duck.

Ancus,-i, 2 *m.*, Ancus(Marcius

ango, -ere, -xi, -ctum, 3 *v. a* I pain, distress; *in pass* I feel pain *or* distressed.

animal, -ālis, 3 *n.*, an animal

animus, -i, 2 *m.*, mind, spirits inclination, courage; bon animo, of good cheer.

annus, -i, 2 *m.*, year.

ante, *prep. with acc.*, before.

anteā, *adv.*, previously, before

antequam, *conj.*, before.

antīquus, -a, -um, *adj.*, old, ancient.

aperio, -īre, -ui, -ertum, 4 *v. a.*, I open.

apertus, -a, -um, *adj.*, open.

Apollo, -inis, 3 *m.*, Apollo.

appello, 1 *v. a.*, I call.

ap-pōno, -ere, -posui, -positum, 3 *v. a.*, I place before, serve.

aptus, -a, -um, *adj.*, suitable, fit (*with dat.*).

apud, *prep. with acc.*, at, among.

aqua, -ae, 1 *f.*, water; *in pl.*, mineral waters, springs.

arātrum, -i, 2 *n.*, a plough.

argentum, -i, 2 *n.*, silver, money.

arma, -ōrum, 2 *n. pl.*, arms, war, fighting.

ars, artis, 3 *f.*, art.
Artemisia, -ae, 1 *f.*, Artemisia.
arx, arcis, 3 *f.*, a citadel.
Ăsia, -ae, 1 *f.*, Asia (originally
    Asia Minor).
ăter, -tra, -trum, *adj.*, black.
ătrium, -i, 2 *n.*, the atrium
    (fore-court *or* hall next to
    the entrance of a Roman
    house).
Attica, -ae, 1 *f.*, Attica.
auctōritas, -ātis, 3 *f.*, authority.
auctumnus, -i, 2 *m.*, autumn.
audācia, -ae, 1 *f.*, boldness.
audio, 4 *v. a.*, I hear, listen.
augeo, -ēre, auxi, auctum,
    2 *v. a.*, I increase.
auris, -is, 3 *f.*, an ear.
aurum, -i, 2 *n.*, gold.
Austrālia, -ae, 1 *f.*, Australia.
Austrālis, -e, *adj.*, southern ;
    Australian.
aut, *conj.*, either, or (aut ex-
    cludes one term, vel makes
    the two indifferent).
autem, *conj.*, but, moreover,
    now (*cannot stand first*).
auxilium, -i, 2 *n.*, help, aid ;
    pred. dat. auxilio, to the
    help of ; *also* auxilio esse,
    to assist.
avus, -i, 2 *m.*, a grandfather.

Babylōn, -ōnis, 3 *f.*, Babylon.
Babylōnius, -a, -um, *adj.*,
    Babylonian.
Baiae, -ārum, 1 *f. pl.*, Baiae.
barbarus, -a, -um, *adj.*, bar-
    barian, foreign.
barbarus, -i, 2 *m.*, a barbarian,
    stranger.
beătus, -a, -um, *adj.*, happy,
    blessed.

bellum, -i, 2 *n.*, war.
bene, *adv.*, well.
Beneventum, -i, 2 *n.*, Bene-
    ventum.
Biās, -antis, 3 *m.*, Bias.
bibo, -ere, bibi, bibitum, 3 *v. a.*,
    I drink.
bonum, -i, 2 *n.*, the good.
bonus, -a, -um, *adj.*, good.
bracchium, -i, 2 *n.*, an arm.
brevi, *adv.*, shortly (*for* brevi
    tempore).
Brundisium, -i, 2 *n.*, Brundi-
    sium.

caeco, 1 *v. a.*, I blind.
caecus, -a, -um, *adj.*, blind.
caedes, -is, 3 *f.*, slaughter.
Caesar, -aris, 3 *m.*, Caesar.
callidus, -a, -um, *adj.*, cunning.
Canada, -ae, 1 *f.*, Canada.
canis, -is, 3 *m. and f.*, a dog
    (*gen. pl.* canum).
Cannae, -ārum, 1 *f. pl.*, Cannae.
Cannensis, -e, *adj.*, of Cannae.
canto, 1 *v. n. and a.*, I sing.
capio, -ere, cēpi, captum, 3 *v. a.*,
    I take, seize.
Capua, -ae, 1 *f.*, Capua.
caput, -pitis, 3 *n.*, a head.
Căria, -ae, 1 *f.*, Caria (a pro-
    vince in Asia Minor).
carmen, -inis, 3 *n.*, a song,
    poem, poetry.
caro, carnis, 3 *f.*, flesh, meat.
Carthāginiensis, -e, *adj.*, Car-
    thaginian.
Carthāgo, -inis, 3 *f.*, Carthage.
cărus, -a, -um, *adj.*, dear.
castra, -ōrum, 2 *n. pl.*, camp.
caupo, -ōnis, 3 *m.*, landlord.
causa, -ae, 1 *f.*, a cause, reason,
    case ; *abl.* causă, for the

sake of (*follows its substantive and refers to the future*).

caveo, -3re, cāvi, cautum, 2 *v. n.*, I beware, take care.

cēdo, -ere, cessi, cessum, 3 *v. a. and n.*, I yield, retreat.

cĕlĕbro, 1 *v. a.*, I throng, celebrate.

celer, -eris, -ere, *adj.*, quick.

celeriter, *adv.*, quickly.

cēlo, 1 *v. a.*, I conceal.

cēna, 1 *f.*, a meal, dinner.

centum, *indecl. num. adj.*, a hundred.

Cerberus, -i, 2 *m.*, Cerberus.

certāmen, -minis, 3 *n.*, a contest.

certiōrem facio, I inform (*lit.* I make more certain).

certo, 1 *v. n.*, I contend, vie with.

cēteri, -ae, -a, *adj.*, the rest, the other.

Cicero, -ōnis, 3 *m.*, Cicero.

Cincinnātus, -i, 2 *m.*, Cincinnatus.

cingo, -ere, cinxi, cinctum, 3 *v. a.*, I surround.

circā, *prep. with acc.*, around.

cīvīlis, -e, *adj.*, pertaining to citizens, civil.

cīvis, -is, 3 *m.*, a citizen.

cīvitas, -ātis, 3 *f.*, a state.

clādes, -is, 3 *f.*, a disaster, defeat, loss.

clāmor, -ōris, 3 *m.*, a shout, cry.

clārus, -a, -um, *adj.*, famous, celebrated.

classis, -is, 3 *f.*, a fleet.

Claudius, -i, 2 *m.*, Claudius.

cognōmen, -inis, 3 *n.*, a surname.

color, -ōris, 3 *m.*, colour.

columna, -ae, 1 *f.*, a colu pillar.

comes, -itis, 3 *m.*, a compan

comitor, -āri, -atus s 1 *v. dep.*, I accompany.

com-mitto, -ere, -mīsi, -n sum, 3 *v. a.*, I commit.

com-moveo, -ēre, -mōvi, -r tum, 2 *v. a.*, I sta begin.

commūnis, -e, *adj.*, comme in common.

com-paro, 1 *v. a.*, I get togeth raise, compare.

com-pleo, -ēre, -plēvi, -plētu 2 *v. a.*, I fill, fill up.

concilium, -i, 2 *n.*, a counc meeting.

condicio, -ōnis, 3 *f.*, conditio terms.

coniunctus, -a, -um, *adj.*, clos united.

cōnor, -āri, -ātus sum, 1 *v. a* I attempt, try.

con-scendo, -ere, -ndi, -nsum 3 *v. a.*, I go on board embark.

con-sīdero, 1 *v. a.*, I examine.

consilio, by stratagem.

consilium, -i, 2 *n.*, a plan stratagem.

con-spicio, -ere, -spexi, -spec tum, 3 *v. a.*, I see, spy.

consul, -ulis, 3 *m.*, a consul.

con-sulto, 1 *v. a.*, I consult, deliberate.

con-sūmo, -ere, -sumpsi, -sumptum, 3 *v. a.*, I consume, waste.

con-temno, -ere, -tempsi, -temptum, 3 *v. a.*, I despise.

con-tendo, -ere, -tendi, -tentum, 3 *v. n.*, I contend, compete.

contentio, -ōnis, 3 *f.*, quarrel, dispute.

contentus, -a, -um, *adj.*, content.

contrā, *prep. with acc.*, against.

convoco, 1 *v. a.*, I call together.

cōpiae, -ārum, 1 *f. pl.*, forces.

corōna, -ae, 1 *f.*, a wreath, crown.

corpus, -poris, 3 *n.*, body.

crās, *adv.*, to-morrow.

cremo, 1 *v. a.*, I burn.

creo, 1 *v. a.*, I create, appoint, elect (*with double acc.*).

crucio, 1 *v. a.*, I torture, distress.

crūdēliter, *adv.*, cruelly.

cubiculum, -i, 2 *n.*, a bedroom.

culpo, 1 *v. a.*, I blame.

cum, *prep. with abl.*, with (cum *follows and is joined to the personal and relative pronouns* mēcum, *&c.*).

cumulo, 1 *v. a.*, I load.

cupīdo, -inis, 3 *f.*, desire.

cupidus, -a, -um, *adj.*, eager, desirous.

cūr, *adv.*, why?

cūra, -ae, 1 *f.*, care; *pred. dat.* cūrae, an object of care.

Curius, -i, 2 *m.*, Curius.

cūro, 1 *v. a.*, I take care of, look after.

curro, -ere, cucurri, cursum, 3 *v. n.*, I run.

currus, -ūs, 4 *m.*, a chariot.

cursus, -ūs, 4 *m.*, running, course.

custōdio, 4 *v. a.*, I guard, protect.

custōs, -ōdis, 3 *m.*, a guard.

Cynicus, -i, 2 *m.*, a Cynic philosopher, a Cynic (*lit.* doglike).

damno, 1 *v. a.*, I condemn, *with gen. of charge*; capitis damno, I condemn to death.

Dārēus, -ii, 2 *m.*, Darius.

dē, *prep. with abl.*, down from, about, concerning, for.

dea, -ae, 1 *f.*, a goddess.

dē-bello, 1 *v. a.*, I vanquish, subdue.

dēbeo, 2 *v. a.*, I owe.

decem, *indecl. num. adj.*, ten; decem-viri, a college of ten men, the decemvirs.

decoro, 1 *v. a.*, I decorate, adorn.

decus, -oris, 3 *n.*, grace, honour; *pred. dat.* decori, a source of honour, an ornament.

dedi, *perf. tense of* do.

dē-fatīgo, 1 *v. a.*, I weary, tire.

dē-fendo, -ere, -di, -sum, 3 *v. a.*, I ward off, defend.

dē-fleo, -ēre, -ēvi, -ētum, 2 *v. a.*, I weep for, lament.

dē-icio, -ere, -iēci, -iectum, 3 *v. a.*, I cast down; deprive, rob of (*with abl. as* spē, hope).

deinde, *adv.*, then, thereupon.

dēlecto, 1 *v. a.*, I delight.

dēlectus, -ūs, 4 *m.*, a levy, recruiting (*of troops*).

dēleo, -ēre, -ēvi, -ētum, 2 *v. a.*, I destroy, blot out.

dē-ligo, -ere, -lēgi, -lectum, 3 *v. a.*, I choose, select.

dēmo, -ere, dempsi, demptum, 3 *v. a.*, I take away.

dē-sero, -ere, -serui, -sertum, 3 *v. a.*, I desert.

dē-signo, 1 *v. a.*, I mark out, choose.

dē-stituo, -ere, -ui, -ūtum, 3 *v. a.*, I desert, disappoint.

dē-struo, -ere, -xi, -ctum, 3 *v. a.*, I destroy.

dē-sum, -esse, -fui, *v. n.*, I am wanting, fail.

dē-terreo, 2 *v. a.*, I frighten, hinder (*with prep.* ab *or* dē, from).

deus, -i, 2 *m.*, a god.

dē-voro, 1 *v. a.*, I devour.

dexter, -tra, -trum, *adj.*, right.

dextra, -ae, 1 *f.*, right hand.

Diāna, -ae, 1 *f.*, Diana.

dīco, -ere, -xi, -ctum, 3 *v. a.*, I say.

dictātūra, -ae, 1 *f.*, the dictatorship.

diēs, -ēi, 5 *m.*, a day.

difficilis, -e, *adj.*, difficult.

dignus, -a, -um, *adj.*, worthy (*with abl.*).

dīligenter, *adv.*, carefully.

dīmidius, -a, -um, *adj.*, half.

Diogenes, -is, *m.*, Diogenes.

dī-rigo, -ere, -rexi, -rectum, 1 *v. a.*, I direct.

dis-cerpo, -ere, -psi, -ptum, 3 *v. a.*, I cut in pieces, carve.

disciplīna, -ae, 1 *f.*, training.

discipulus, -i, 2 *m.*, a pupil.

dissimilis, -e, *adj.*, unlike.

diū, *adv.*, for a long time.

dīversus, -a, -um, *adj.*, different.

dī-vido, -ere, -vīsi, -vīsum, 3 *v. a.*, I divide.

dīvitiae, -ārum, 1 *f. pl.*, ri

do, dare, dedi, datum, 1 I give, pay, suffer.

doceo, -ēre, -cui, -ctum, 2 I teach.

dolor, -ōris, 3 *m.*, pain, gr

dolus, -i, 2 *m.*, cunning.

domina, -ae, 1 *f.*, lady, s reign.

dominus, -i, 2 *m.*, lord, ma

domus, -ūs, 4 *f.*, a hou domī, at home.

dōnum, -i, 2 *n.*, a gift.

dubius, -a, -um, *adj.*, doubt dangerous.

ducenti, -ae, -a, *num. adj.*, hundred.

dūco, -ere, -xi, -ctum, 3 *v.* I lead.

Duilius, -i, 2 *m.*, Duilius.

dulcis, -e, *adj.*, sweet.

dum, *conj.*, while.

duo, duae, duo, *num. adj.*, t

duodecim, *num. adj.*, twelve

duodēvīgintī, *num. adj.*, eig een.

dūrus, -a, -um, *adj.*, hard.

dux, ducis, 3 *m.*, a lead general.

ē, *prep. with abl.*, from, o of.

ecce, *interj.*, lo ! *or* behol here is !

ēduco, 1 *v. a.*, I bring up, ed cate.

ego, 1 *pers. pron.*, I.

ēheu, *interj.*, alas !

elementa, -ōrum, 2 *n. pl.*, el ments, rudiments.

ē-ligo, -ere, -lēgi, -lectum 3 *v. a.*, I choose, elect.

ēloquentia, -ae, 1 *f.*, eloquenc

ē-mendo, 1 *v. a.*, I free from faults, correct, improve.

enim, *conj.*, for (*cannot stand first*).

eo, īre, īvi *or* ii, itum, *v. n.*, I go.

eō, *adv.* (*with words of comparison*), so much, by so much.

Ephesius, -a, -um, *adj.*, Ephesian.

Epicūrēus, -a, -um, *adj.*, Epicurean.

Epicūrus, -i, 2 *m.*, Epicurus.

epistola, -ae, 1 *f.*, a letter.

eques, -itis, 3 *m.*, a horseman, *in plur.*, cavalry.

equus, -i, 2 *m.*, a horse; currus equis iungitur, the horses are harnessed to the chariot.

ē-ripio, -ere, -ripui, -reptum, 3 *v. a.*, I snatch out, destroy.

erro, 1 *v. n.*, I err, make a mistake, wander.

ē-rudio, 4 *v. a.*, I train, teach.

et, *conj.*, and ; et . . . et, both . . . and.

etiam, *adv.*, also, even.

Ētrūria, -ae, 1 *f.*, Etruria.

ex, *prep. with abl.*, out of (*always used before vowels, and more common than* ē *even before consonants*).

ex-animo, 1 *v. a.*, I deprive of life, terrify.

excito, 1 *v. a.*, I arouse, inflame.

exemplum, -i, 2 *n.*, an example.

ex-eo, -īre, -ii, -itum, *v. n.*, I go out, leave.

ex-erceo, 2 *v. a.*, I train, exercise.

exercitus, -ūs, 4 *m.*, an army.

exitium, -i, 2 *n.*, destruction.

exordium, -i, 2 *n.*, commencement.

ex-pedio, 4 *v. a.*, I set free, arrange, make ready, release, open up.

ex-plico, -āre, -āvi *and* -ui, -atum *and* -itum, 1 *v. a.*, I explain, unfold.

ex-plōro, 1 *v. a.*, I search out, examine.

ex-pugno, 1 *v. a.*, I storm, capture.

ex-specto, 1 *v. a.*, I wait for, await.

ex-stinguo, -ere, -stinxi, -stinctum, 3 *v. a.*, I quench, blot out, extinguish.

Fābricius, -i, 2 *m.*, Fabricius.

fābula, -ae, 1 *f.*, a tale, story.

facilis, -e, *adj.*, easy.

facinus, -oris, 3 *n.*, a deed ; *esp.* a bad deed, crime.

facio, -ere, fēci, factum, 3 *v. a.*, I do, make.

factio, -ōnis, 3 *f.*, a side, faction, party.

factum, -i, 2 *n.*, a deed.

fāma, -ae, 1 *f.*, fame, report.

fauces, -ium, 3 *f. pl.*, passage, corridor.

fēlīcitas, -ātis, 3 *f.*, good fortune, luck.

fēlīciter, *adv.*, happily, luckily.

fēmina, -ae, 1 *f.*, a woman.

fenestra, -ae, 1 *f.*, a window.

ferula, -ae, 1 *f.*, a whip, rod (*for slaves or boys*).

fessus, -a, -um, *adj.*, weary.

fides, -ei, 5 *f.*, faith, loyalty ; fidem praesto, I keep my word; **fidem habeo** (*with dat.*), I have faith in.

fides, -ium, 3 *f. plur.*, a harp, lute; **fidibus canto,** I sing to the lute.

fidus, -a, -um, *adj.*, faithful.

figūra, -ae, 1 *f.*, a figure. statue.

fīlius, -i, 2 *m.*, a son.

fīnio, 4 *v. a.*, I finish.

fīnis, -is, 3 *m.*, an end.

firmo, 1 *v. a.*, I make strong, strengthen.

firmus, -a, -um, *adj.*, strong.

flecto, -ere, -xi, -xum, 3 *v. a.*, I bend, turn.

foedus, -eris, 3 *n.*, a treaty.

forma, -ae, 1 *f.*, shape, grace, beauty.

fortasse, *adv.*, perhaps.

fortis, -e, *adj.*, brave.

fortitūdo, -inis, 3 *f.*, courage, bravery.

fortūna, -ae, 1 *f.*, fortune.

fossa, -ae, 1 *f.*, a ditch.

frāter, frātris, 3 *m.*, brother.

fraus, -dis, 3 *f.*, a trick, deceit.

frigidus, -a, -um, *adj.*, cold.

frons, -ntis, 3 *f.*, a brow, forehead.

frūgālitas, -ātis, 3 *f.*, frugality.

frūmentum, -i, 2 *n.*, corn.

frustrā, *adv.*, in vain.

frustror, -āri, -ātus sum, 1 *v. dep.*, I frustrate, destroy.

fuga, -ae, 1 *f.*, flight.

fugio, -ere, fūgi, fugitum, 3 *v. n.*, I fly.

fugo, 1 *v. a.*, I put to flight, rout.

fundo, -ere, fūdi, fūsum, 3 *v. a.*, I pour, pour out.

fundus, -i, 2 *m.*, a farm.

fūnus, -eris, 3 *n.*, fun burial, death.

furor, -ōris, 3 *m.*, rage, ness.

Gāius, *gen.* Gāi, 2 *m.*, Gai

gallīna, -ae, 1 *f.*, a hen.

gaudeo, -ēre, gāvīsus 2 *v. n.*, I am glad, rejo

gaudium, -ii, 2 *n.*, joy.

gens, gentis, 3 *f.*, a race, tr

genus, -eris, 3 *n.*, a kind, r

gero, -ere, gessi, gestum, 3 *v* I carry on, wage (*w* morem gero, I com with (*with dat. of pers*

glōria, -ae, 1 *f.*, glory, fam

Graecia, -ae, 1 *f.*, Greece.

Graecus, -a, -um, *adj.*, Gree

grātia, -ae, 1 *f.*, thanks; grāt ago, I give thanks; g tiam habeo, I feel gratef

Grātiae, -ārum, 2 *f. pl.*, t Graces.

grātus, -a, -um, *adj.*, pleasa grateful.

gravis, -e, *adj.*, heavy, seriou disastrous.

gravitas, -ātis, 3 *f.*, heavines weight, dignity.

graviter, *adv.*, heavily, se ously.

guberno, 1 *v. a.*, I steer, direc govern.

gymnasium, -i, 2 *n.*, a gyn nasium, school for exe cise.

habeo, 2 *v. a.*, I have, hold habeo grātiam, I an grateful; habeo delec tum, I hold a levy (*o* *troops*); res se habent matters stand *or* are situated.

habito, 1 *v. n.,* I dwell, live.

Hannibal, -alis, 3 *m.,* Hannibal.

Helena, -ae, 1 *f.,* Helena.

Hercules, -is, 3 *m.,* Hercules.

heus, *interj.,* ho there ! hark ! holloa !

hīc, *adv.,* in this place, here.

hīc, haec, hōc, *pron. demonstr.,* this ; he, she, it ; the latter.

hiems, -emis, 3 *f.,* winter.

hilaris, -e, *adj.,* merry, jovial.

hinc, *adv.,* from this place, hence.

Hispānia, -ae, 1 *f.,* Spain.

hodiē, *adv.,* on this day, to-day.

Homērus, -i, 2 *m.,* Homer.

homo, -inis, 3 *m. and f.,* a human being, a man.

honestas, -ātis, 3 *f.,* honesty.

honestus, -a, -um, *adj.,* honourable.

honor, -ōris, 3 *m.,* honour ; honōris causā, out of respect, in order to show honour.

hōra, -ae, 1 *f.,* hour ; ad hōram, to the hour, punctually.

Horātius, -i, 2 *m.,* Horatius.

horridus, -a, -um, *adj.,* rough, savage.

hortus, -i, 2 *m.,* a garden, *in sing. generally of a* kitchen-garden, *in plur. of a* pleasure-garden.

hospes, -itis, 3 *m.,* a guest.

hostis, -is, 3 *m.,* an enemy.

hūc, *adv.,* hither.

hūmānus, -a, -um, *adj.,* natural to man.

humilis, -e, *adj.,* humble, lowly.

iaculum, -i, 2 *n.,* a dart, javelin.

iam, *adv.,* now, already ; non iam, no longer.

Iānus, -i, 2 *m.,* Janus.

ibī, *adv.,* there, in that place.

id temporis, *adverbial,* at that time.

īdem, eadem, idem, *pron.,* the same ; īdem qui, the same as.

igitur, *conj.,* therefore, then.

ignāvia, -ae, 1 *f.,* idleness, cowardice.

ignis, -is, 3 *m.,* fire.

ignōro, 1 *v. a.,* I am ignorant, do not know.

ille, illa, illud, *pron.,* that ; he, she, it ; the former ; *with name of a person,* the famous (*follows the noun*).

illūc, *adv.,* to that place, thither.

imber, -bris, 3 *m.,* rain, storm.

imitor, -āri, -ātus sum, 1 *v. dep.,* I imitate.

impedio, 4 *v. a.,* I hinder, prevent.

imperātor, -ōris, 3 *m.,* a general ; *also,* a Roman emperor.

imperium, -i, 2 *n.,* rule, command, government, empire.

imperītus, -a, -um, *adj.,* unskilled.

impetro, 1 *v. a.,* I obtain (by request).

impetus, -ūs, 4 *m.,* an attack ; impetum do, I make an attack.

im-pleo, -ēre, -ēvi, -ētum, 2 *v. a.,* I fill, fill up.

impluvium, -i, 2 *n.,* a skylight ; impluvium (*the opening in* *roof of a Roman atrium, through which the smoke escaped ; hence, also, the square basin which received the rain).*

im-pōno, -ere, -posui, -positum, 3 *v. a.*, I put *or* set upon ; finem bello impōno, I put an end to the war.

im-porto, 1 *v. a.*, I bring in, import.

improbus, -a, -um, *adj.*, wicked.

in, *prep. with abl.*, in, on, upon, at.

in, *prep. with acc.*, into, to, on.

incendium, -i, 2 *n.*, a fire, conflagration.

incendo, -ere, -di, -sum, 3 *v. a.*, I set on fire, kindle.

in-cito, 1 *v. a.*, I urge on, encourage.

incola, -ae, 1 *m.*, an inhabitant.

incommodum, -i, 2 *n.*, disaster, misfortune.

incursio, -ōnis, 3 *f.*, an attack, invasion.

in-dīco, -ere, -xi, -ctum, 3 *v. a.*, I declare ; bellum indīco, I declare war upon (*with dat. of person*).

in-eo, -īre, -ii, -itum, *v. n. and a.*, I enter, enter upon.

infrā, *adv.*, below, lower down.

ingens, -entis, *adj.*, huge, immense.

inimīcus, -a, -um, *adj.*, hostile.

inimīcus, -i, 2 *m.*, an enemy.

initium, -i, 2 *n.*, beginning.

iniūria, -ae, 1 *f.*, injury, wrong, insult.

insidiae, -ārum, 1 *f. pl.*, an ambush.

in-stituo, -ere, -ui, -ūtum, 3 *v. a.*,

I train, instruct (*abl.*).

in-struo, -ere, -xi, -ctum, 3 I draw up.

insula, -ae, 1 *f.*, an island.

integritas, -ātis, 3 *f.*, integ

inter, *prep. with acc.*, betw among.

inter-pōno, -ere, -posui, -p tum, 3 *v. a.*, I interp let pass, leave (*an inter*

intro, 1 *v. a.*, I enter.

invītus, -a, -um, *adj.*, unv ing.

iocōsus, -a, -um, *adj.*, hun ous, funny.

ipse, ipsa, ipsum, *pron. de* self, in person, hims herself.

ira, -ae, 1 *f.*, anger.

irrīto, 1 *v. a.*, I provoke, inci

is, ea, id, *pron. dem.*, he, sl it, that.

iste, ista, istud, *pron. de* that near you, that yours.

ita, *adv.*, so thus.

Ītalia, -ae, 1 *f.*, Italy.

itaque, *conj.*, and so, thus.

iter, itineris, 3 *n.*, a journe march, road.

iterum, *adv.*, again.

iūcundus, -a, -um, *adj.*, ple sant.

iūdex, -icis, 3 *m.*, a judge.

iūdicium, -i, 2 *n.*, a jud ment, trial.

iūdico, 1 *v. a.*, I judge.

iungo, -ere, -xi, -ctum, 3 *v. a.* I join, form ; equis cur rum iungo, I harness th horses to the chariot.

Iuppiter Iovis, 3 *m.*, Jupiter

iūs, iūris, 3 *n.*, law, right.

iuvo, -āre, iūvi, iūtum, 3 *v. a.*, I help, assist.

labor, -ōris, 3 *m.*, labour, work.

lac, lactis, 3 *n.*, milk.

laetor, -āri, -ātus sum, 1 *v. dep.*, I rejoice.

lāna, -ae, 1 *f.*, wool.

Latīnus, -a, -um, *adj.*, Latin.

lătro, -ōnis, 3 *m.*, a robber.

lātus, -a, -um, *adj.*, broad.

laudo, 1 *v. a.*, I praise.

laus, laudis, 3 *f.*, praise.

lavo, -āre, lāvi, lavātum (*perf. part.* lautus), 1 *v. a.*, I wash.

lectus, -i, 2 *m.*, a bed, couch (*for reclining on at meals*).

legio, -ōnis, 3 *f.*, a legion.

lego, -ere, lēgi, lectum, 3 *v. a.*, I choose, read.

lēnio, 4 *v. a.*, I soften, soothe.

Leōnidas, -ae, 1 *m.*, Leonidas.

levis, -e, *adj.*, light.

lex, lēgis, 3 *f.*, a law.

libenter, *adv.*, willingly, gladly.

liber, -bri, 2 *m.*, a book.

līberi, -ōrum, 2 *m. pl.*, children.

lībero, 1 *v. a.*, I set free (*with abl. of thing freed from*).

libet, -ere, lĭbuit *and* libitum est, 2 *v. n. and impers.*, it pleases.

līmen, -inis, 3 *n.*, a threshold.

lingua, -ae, 1 *f.*, tongue, language.

linteum, -i, 2 *n.*, linen-cloth *or* towel.

līnum, -i, 2 *n.*, flax, linen-cloth *or* garment.

litterae, -ārum, 2 *f. pl.*, letters, literature.

litterārius, -a, -um, *adj.*, of reading and writing ; lūdus litterārius, an elementary school.

lītus, -oris, 3 *n.*, a shore.

locus, -i, 2 *m.*, place, room (*in plur.* loci, *m.*, single places; loca, *n.*, connected places, region); *abl.*, loco, in place of, instead of.

longē, *adv.*, far, very.

longus, -a, -um, *adj.*, long.

lūdi, -ōrum, 2 *m. pl.*, games.

lūdo, -ere, -si, -sum, 3 *v. a. and n.*, I play, mock.

lūdus, -i, 2 *m.*, a school (*for young children*).

lūsus, -ūs, 4 *m.*, a game.

luxuria, -ae, 1 *f.*, luxury.

luxuriōsus, -a, -um, *adj.*, luxurious, extravagant.

Macedones, -um, 3 *m. pl.*, the Macedonians.

magis, *comp. adv.*, more, rather.

magnopere, *adv.*, greatly.

magnus, -a, -um, *adj.*, great, large.

māior, -us, *comp. adj.*, greater.

male, *adv.*, badly, ill.

mālo, malle, mālui, *v. a. and n.*, I prefer.

malum, -i, 2 *n.*, an ill, misfortune.

mando, 1 *v. a.*, I entrust, commit ; memoriae mando, I hand down to posterity.

māne, *adv.*, in the morning.

maneo, -ēre, -nsi, -nsum, 2 *v. n.*, I remain ; promisso maneo, I keep a promise.

Mānes, -ium, 3 *m. pl.,* the departed spirits, ghosts *or* shades.

manus, -ūs, 4 *f.,* a hand.

Marcius, -i, 2 *m.,* Marcius.

mare, maris, 3 *n.,* the sea.

maritimus, -a, -um, *adj.,* of the sea, maritime, naval.

marītus, -i, 2 *m.,* a husband.

Marius, -i, 2 *m.,* Marius.

marmoreus, -a, -um, *adj.,* of marble.

māter, -tris, 3 *f.,* mother.

Mausōlus, -i, 2 *m.,* Mausolus.

maximē, *sup. adv.,* very greatly, especially.

maximus, -a, -um, *sup. adj.,* very great, greatest.

Mēdi, -ōrum, 2 *m. pl.,* the Medes.

medius, -a, -um, *adj.,* middle.

melior, -us, *comp. adj.,* better.

memor, *gen.* memoris, *adj.,* mindful (*with gen.*).

memoria, -ae, 1 *f.,* memory.

mendīcus, -i, 2 *m.,* a beggar.

mens, mentis, 3 *f.,* mind.

mensa, -ae, 1 *f.,* a table ; mena secunda, dessert.

mensis, -is, 3 *m.,* month.

mereor, -ēri, meritus sum, 2 *v. dep.,* I deserve.

metus, -ūs, 4 *m.,* fear.

mīgro, 1 *v. a.,* I migrate, depart.

mīles, -itis, 3 *m.,* soldier.

mīlia, *n. pl.,* thousands.

mille, *num. adj. indecl.,* thousand.

minimus, -a, -um, *sup. adj.,* least, smallest.

minister, -tri, 2 *m.,* servant, attendant.

ministro, 1 *v. a.,* I wait hand, serve.

minor, -us, *comp. adj.,* small inferior.

Mīnos, -ōis, 3 *m.,* Minos.

minus, *comp. adv.,* less.

mirāculum, -i, 2 *n.,* a wond

mirus, -a, -um, *adj.,* stran; wonderful.

misceo, -ere, miscui, mixtu. 2 *v. a.,* I mix (*with wate*

mitto, -ere, mīsi, missu 3 *v. a.,* I send.

moderor, -āri, -ātus su 1 *v. dep.,* I rule, govern.

modo, *adv.,* only, just.

modus, -i, 2 *m.,* way, manne

moenia, -ium, 3 *n. pl.,* tow walls.

mōles, -is, 3 *f.,* dam, works.

molestus, -a, -um, *adj.,* troubl some.

mollio, 4 *v. a.,* I soften, sooth

mollitia, -ae, 1 *f.,* softness.

moneo, 2 *v. a.,* I advise, warr

mons, montis, 3 *m.,* a hill mountain.

monstro, 1 *v. a.,* I show.

monumentum, -i, 2 *n.,* a build ing, monument.

mora, -ae, 1 *f.,* delay.

morior, mori, mortuus sum, 3 *v. dep.,* I die.

mors, mortis, 3 *f.,* death.

mortui, -ōrum, 2 *m. pl.,* the dead.

mortuus, -a, -um, *adj.,* dead.

mōs, mōris, 3 *m.,* custom, manner; *in plur.,* morals; morem gero, I comply with (*with dat. of pers.*).

moveo, -ēre, mōvi, mōtum, 2 *v. a.,* I move.

mox, *adv.*, soon.

multum, *adv.*, much.

multus, -a, -um, *adj.*, much; *in pl.*, many.

mundus, -i, 2 *m.*, the world.

mūnio, 4 *v. a.*, I fortify.

mūnus, -eris, 3 *n.*, a gift, present.

mūraena, -ae, 1 *f.*, a muraena, sea-water eel.

mūrus, -i, 2 *m.*, a wall.

Mūsa, -ae, 1 *f.*, a Muse.

mūto, 1 *v. a.*, I change.

nam, *conj.*, for.

narro, 1 *v. a.*, I relate.

nātūra, -ae, 1 *f.*, nature.

nāvigo, 1 *v. n.*, I sail.

nāvis, -is, 3 *f.*, a ship.

Neāpolis, -is, 3 *f.*, Naples.

nec, *conj.*, nor; nec . . . nec, *or* neque . . . neque (*before vowels*), neither . . . nor.

necesse, *neutr. adj.*, *acc. and nom.*, necessary.

neco, 1 *v. a.*, I kill.

neglego, 3 *v. a.*, I neglect.

negōtium, -i, 2 *n.*, business, trouble.

nēmo, *m. and f.*, nobody (*acc.* nēminem, *dat.* nēmini; *for gen. and abl.* nullīus *and* nullo, nullā *are used*).

nempe, *conj.*, doubtless, to be sure.

neque, *conj.*, and not, neither, nor; *also see* nec.

nihil, *n. indecl.*, nothing.

Nīlus, -i, 2 *m.*, the Nile.

nimis, *adv.*, too much.

nisi, *conj.*, if not, unless.

nītor, nīti, nīsus *or* nixus sum, 3 *v. dep.*, I strive.

nōlo, nolle, nōlui, *v. irreg. a. and n.*, I am unwilling, not do wish.

nōmen, -inis, 3 *n.*, a name.

nōmino, 1 *v. a.*, I name, call, appoint.

nōn, *adv.*, not; non iam, no longer; nondum, not yet.

nonne, *interrog. adv.*, not?

noster, -tra, -trum, *possess. pron.*, our.

nōtus, -a, -um, *adj.*, known.

novem, *num. adj.*, nine.

num, *an interrog. particle*, expecting a negative answer.

Nūma, -ae, 1 *m.*, Numa.

numerus, -i, 2 *m.*, number.

nunc, *adv.*, now.

nunquam, *adv.*, never.

nuntio, 1 *v. a.*, I announce, report.

nūtrio, 4 *v. a.*, I nourish, support.

Ō, *interj.*, O! Oh!

ob, *prep. with acc.*, on account of, for.

ob-sideo, -ēre, -sēdi, -sessum, 2 *v. a.*, I besiege, blockade.

ōceanus, -i, 2 *m.*, the ocean.

octingenti, -ae, -a, *num. adj.*, eight hundred.

oculus, -i, 2 *m.*, an eye.

ōlim, *adv.*, formerly, once.

olīva, -ae, 1 *f.*, olive.

Olympias, -adis, 3 *f.*, an Olympiad.

Olympius, -a, -um, *adj.*, Olympian.

omnis, -e, *adj.*, all, every.

onero, 1 *v. a.*, I load, burden.

onus, -eris, 3 *n.*, a burden.

operārius, -a, -um, *adj.*, of *or*

belonging to labour, working.

oppidum, -i, 2 *n.,* a town.

op-primo, -ere, -pressi, -pressum, 3 *v. a.,* I overwhelm, overcome.

op-pugno, 1 *v. a.,* I attack.

optimus, -a, -um, *sup. adj.,* best.

opto, 1 *v. a.,* I wish, desire.

opulentus, -a, -um, *adj.,* rich.

opus, -eris, 3 *n.,* work, labour; quid opus est, what need is there? (*with abl. of thing needed*).

ōrātor, -ōris, 3 *m.,* an orator, speaker.

orbis, -is, 3 *m.,* a circle ; *hence* orbis *or* orbis terrarum, the world.

ornāmentum, -i, 2 *n.,* ornament.

ornātus, -a, -um, *adj.,* adorned.

orno, 1 *v. a.,* I adorn, decorate.

ostium, -i, 2 *n.,* a door.

ostrea, -ae, 1 *f.,* an oyster.

ovis, -is, 3 *f.,* a sheep.

paedagōgus, -i, 2 *m.,* a preceptor (*slave who took the children to school and looked after them at home*).

paene, *adv.,* almost.

palaestra, -ae, 1 *f.,* a wrestling-school, palaestra (*for youths, while the gymnasium was for older people*).

palūs, -ūdis, 3 *f.,* a marsh.

pānis, -is, 3 *m.,* bread (*gen. pl.* pānum).

pār, paris, *adj.,* equal to, a match for (*with dat.*).

pāreo, 2 *v. n.,* I obey (*with dat.*).

paro, 1 *v. a.,* I prepare, ma ready, gain, win.

pars, partis, 3 *f.,* a part.

partior, -īri, -ītus sum, 4 *v. de* I share, divide.

parum, *subst. indecl. and ad* too little, not enough.

patria, -ae, 1 *f.,* native-lan country.

paucus, -a, -um, *adj.,* few.

paulisper, *adv.,* for a litt while, for a short time.

paululum, *adv.,* a little, trifle.

paupertas, -ātis, 3 *f.,* povert

pax, pācis, 3 *f.,* peace.

pecūnia, -ae, 1 *f.,* money.

pēior, -us, *comp. adj.,* worse.

pellis, -is, 3 *f.,* a skin.

pello, -ere, pepuli, pulsun 3 *v. a.,* I drive, banish.

pendeo, -ēre, pependi, 2 *v. n* I hang, hang down.

penes, *prep. with acc.,* in th power of, with.

per, *prep. with acc.,* through over.

per-dūco, -ere, -xi, -ctum 3 *v. a.,* I lead through bring.

per-erro, 1 *v. a.,* I wander over

perīculum, -i, 2 *n.,* danger.

peristȳlium, -i, 2 *n.,* a peri style (*open court surrounded with columns*).

perniciōsus, -a, -um, *adj.,* destructive.

perpetuus, -a, -um, *adj.,* continuous, constant.

Persae, -ārum, 1 *m. pl.,* the Persians.

per-turbo, 1 *v. a.,* I disturb, confuse.

pēs, pedis, 3 *m.*, a foot; **pedibus īre,** to go on foot.

pessimus, -a, -um, *sup. adj.,* worst.

Pharsālus, -i, 2 *f.,* Pharsalus.

Pharus, -i, 2 *f.,* the light-house (on the island of Pharos).

Phīdias, -ae, 1 *m.,* Phidias.

philosophus, -i, 2 *m.,* a philosopher.

pila, -ae, 1 *f.,* a ball.

pingo, -ere, pinxi, pictum, 3 *v. a.,* I paint, depict.

piscīna, -ae, 1 *f.,* a fish-pond.

placeo, 2 *v. n.,* I please (*with dat.*).

plēnus, -a, -um, *adj.,* full, filled with (*with gen. or abl.*).

plūrimus, -a, -um, *sup. adj.,* very many, most.

plūs, plūris, *neut. comp. adj.,* more; **pluris aestimo,** I value at a higher price.

pōculum, -i, 2 *n.,* a cup, goblet.

poena, -ae, 1 *f.,* punishment, penalty; **poenas do,** I pay the penalty.

Poeni, -ōrum, 2 *m. pl.,* the Carthaginians.

poēta, -ae, 1 *m.,* a poet.

Polyphēmus, -i, 2 *m.,* Polyphemus.

Pompēii, -ōrum, 2 *m. pl.,* Pompeii.

Pompilius, -i, 2 *m.,* Pompilius.

pōmum, -i, 2 *n.,* fruit; apple.

pondus, -eris, 3 *n.,* a weight.

pōno, -ere, posui, positum, 3 *v. a.,* I place, put.

populus, -i, 2 *m.,* the people.

porta, -ae, 1 *f.,* a door, gate.

porto, 1 *v. a.,* I bring, carry.

portus, -ūs, 4 *m.,* a harbour.

possum, posse, potui, *v. n.,* I am able, can, am powerful.

post, *prep. with acc.,* after, behind.

posteā, *adv.,* afterwards, after.

posterus, -a, -um, *adj.,* next.

postīcum, -i, 2 *n.,* a back-door.

postquam, *conj.,* after.

postrīdiē, *adv.,* on the next day.

postulo, 1 *v. a.,* I demand, ask.

potestas, -ātis, 3 *f.,* power.

praebeo, 2 *v. a.,* I show, provide, lend, supply.

praeceptum, -i, 2 *n.,* an example.

praeclārus, -a, -um, *adj.,* famous.

praeda, -ae, 1 *f.,* booty.

praedico, 1 *v. a.,* I praise, extol.

praemium, -i, 2 *n.,* a prize, reward.

praescriptum, -i, 2 *n.,* a lesson, task.

praesidium, -i, 2 *n.,* help, protection.

praestans, -antis, *adj.,* excellent.

preces, -um, 3 *f. pl.,* prayers.

prīmō, *adv.,* at first.

prīmus, -a, -um, *adj.,* first.

princeps, -ipis, 3 *m.,* chief, prince.

prior, -us, *comp. adj.,* former, first.

Priscus, -i, 2 *m.,* Priscus.

prīvātus, -a, -um, *adj.,* private.

prō, *prep. with abl.,* for, on behalf of.

probitas, -ātis, 3 *f.,* goodness, modesty.

probrum, -i, 2 *n.,* insult.

prōd-eo, -īre, -ii, -itum, *v. n.,* I go forth.

proelium, -i, 2 *n.*, a battle.

proficiscor, -i, -fectus sum, 3 *v. dep.*, I set out.

prŏ-flīgo, 1 *v. a.*, I strike down, overthrow.

pro-hibeo, 2 *v. a.*, I shut out.

prōmissum, -i, 2 *n.*, a promise.

prope, *prep. with acc.*, near.

propero, 1 *v. n.*, I hasten.

propitius, -a, -um, *adj.*, propitious, favourable, kind.

proprius, -a, -um, *adj.*, peculiar to, private.

propter, *prep. with acc.*, on account of.

proximus, -a, -um, *sup. adj.*, nearest, next.

publicus, -a, -um, *adj.*, public.

puella, -ae, 1 *f.*, a girl.

puer, -eri, 2 *m.*, a boy, young man; attendant, slave.

pugna, -ae, 1 *f.*, a battle.

pugno, 1 *v. n.*, I fight.

pulcher, -chra, -chrum, *adj.*, beautiful.

pulchritūdo, -inis, 3 *f.*, beauty.

pulso, 1 *v. a.*, I knock.

Pūnicus, -a, -um, *adj.*, Punic, Carthaginian.

pūnio, 4 *v. a.*, I punish.

Puteoli, -ōrum, 2 *m. pl.*, Puteoli.

puto, 1 *v. a.*, I think.

quădrăgintă, *num. adj.*, forty.

quădrīgae, -ārum, 1 *f. pl.*, a four-horsed chariot.

quam, *adv.*, how, how much; tam . . . quam, so much . . . as; *with an adj.*, how; *after comparatives*, than.

quam-ob-rem, *adv.*, wherefore.

quamquam, *conj.*, although.

quandō, *adv.*, when?

quartus, -a, -um, *ord. ad* fourth.

quartus decimus, -a, -um, *or adj.*, fourteenth.

quattuor, *num. adj.*, four.

que, *conj.*, and (*joined to t. latter of two objects whi it connects*).

quī, quae, quod, *rel. and interro pron.*, who, which, what.

quia, *conj.*, because.

quid, *neut. pron.*, what.

quingenti, -ae, -a, *num. adj* five hundred.

quinquăgintă, *num. adj.*, fifty.

quinque, *num. adj.*, five.

quintus, -a, -um, *ord. adj.*, fifth

quis, quis, quid, *interrog. pron.* who? which? what?

quō, *adv.*, whither?

quō, *adv.*, by how much; se eō, *adv.*

quod, *conj.*, because.

quō-modo, *adv.*, how? in what manner?

quondam, *adv.*, formerly, once.

quoque, *adv.*, also.

quot, *indecl. adj.*, how many?

quotīdiē, *adv.*, daily.

rapio, -ere, rapui, raptum, 3 *v. a.*, I seize, carry off.

rapto, 1 *v. a.*, I drag off, seize.

rārus, -a, -um, *adj.*, rare, few.

re-cito, 1 *v. a.*, I recite, relate.

re-cordor, -āri, -ātus sum, 1 *v. dep.*, I recall.

rectē, *adv.*, rightly.

rectus, -a, -um, *adj.*, straight.

red-do, -ere, red-didi, red-ditum, 3 *v. a.*, I restore, make, render.

red-eo, -īre, -ii, -itum, *v. n.*,
   I return, go back.
re-dūco, -ere, -xi, -ctum, 3 *v. a.*,
   I lead back.
rēgīna, -ae, 1 *f.*, queen.
regio, -ōnis, 3 *f.*, region, district.
regnum, -i, 2 *n.*, a kingdom.
rego, -ere, rexi, rectum, 3 *v. a.*,
   I rule.
rēgula, -ae, 1 *f.*, a rule.
Rēgulus, -i, 2 *m.*, Regulus.
religio, -ōnis, 3 *f.*, piety, reli-
   gion, religious scruples.
re-moveo, -ēre, -mōvi, -mōtum,
   2 *v. a.*, I remove, set aside.
re-perio, -īre, rep-peri, repertum, 4 *v. a.*, I find,
   discover.
re-pleo, -ēre, -plēvi, -plētum,
   2 *v. a.*, I fill again, fill
   up.
re-porto, 1 *v. a.*, I bring back,
   gain, win.
re-pudio, 1 *v. a.*, I reject, refuse.
rēs, rei, 5 *f.*, a thing, circum-
   stance, reason, matter.
res adversae, adversity.
responsum, -i, 2 *n.*, an answer.
res publica, the republic, state
   (*declined in both parts*).
res secundae, prosperity.
re-tracto, 1 *v. a.*, I go over
   again, revise.
re-voco, 1 *v. a.*, I call back,
   recall.
rex, rēgis, 3 *m.*, king.
rīpa, -ae, 1 *f.*, a bank (of river).
rogo, 1 *v. a.*, I ask.
Rōma, -ae, 1 *f.*, Rome.
Rōmānus, -a, -um, *adj.*, Roman.
Rōmulus, -i, 2 *m.*, Romulus.
rūre, from the country.
rūri, in the country.

rūs, rūris, 3 *n.*, the country
   (*opp. to town*).
rusticus, -a, -um, *adj.*, rustic,
   rural.

Sabīni, -ōrum, 2 *m. pl.*, the
   Sabines.
saepe, *adv.*, often.
saevus, -a, -um, *adj.*, fierce,
   cruel.
Saguntum, -i, 2 *n.*, Saguntum.
saltus, -ūs, 4 *m.*, jumping,
   leaping.
salūs, -ūtis, 3 *f.*, safety ; *pred.
   dat.*, saluti, a means of
   safety, help.
salvē, good-day ! hail !
salveo, 2 *v. n.*, I am well.
Samnītes, -ium, 3 *m. pl.*, the
   Samnites.
sanctus, -a, -um, *adj.*, hallowed,
   holy.
sānus, -a, -um, *adj.*, healthy.
sapiens, -entis, *adj.*, wise.
sapientia, -ae, 1 *f.*, wisdom.
satelles, -itis, 3 *m.*, an attendant.
satio, 1 *v. a.*, I sate, satisfy.
satis, *adv.*, sufficient, enough.
scelus, -eris, 3 *n.*, a crime.
schola, -ae, 1 *f.*, a school.
scindo, -ere, scidi, scissum,
   3 *v. a.*, I cut, carve.
Scīpio, -ōnis, 3 *m.*, Scipio.
scrībendum, -i, 2 *n.*, writing
   (*a gerund not used in nom.*).
scrībo, -ere, scripsi, scriptum,
   3 *v. a.*, I write.
scriptor, -ōris, 3 *m.*, a writer.
scriptum, -i, 2 *n.*, a writing.
sē *or* sēsē, *reflex. pron.*, himself,
   herself, itself, themselves.
secundō, *adv.*, secondly.
secundus, -a, -um, *adj.*, second,

prosperous, favourable; secunda mensa, dessert; secundae res, prosperity.

sed, *conj.,* but.

Semīramis, -is *or* **-idis,** 3 *f.,* Semiramis.

semper, *adv.,* always.

senātus, -ūs, 4 *m.,* the senate.

senex, -is, 3 *m.,* old-man (*gen. plur.* senum).

sensus, -ūs, 4 *m.,* a sense (*of the body*).

sententia, -ae, 1 *f.,* opinion.

sentio, -īre, sensi, sensum, 4 *v. a.,* I feel, think.

sē-paro, 1 *v. a.,* I separate.

septem, *num. adj.,* seven.

septimus, -a, -um, *ord. adj.,* seventh.

sepulcrum, -i, 2 *n.,* tomb, sepulchre.

sequor, -i, secūtus sum, 3 *v. dep.,* I follow.

sērius, -a, -um, *adj.,* serious.

sērō, *adv.,* late, too late.

servio, 4 *v. n.,* I serve, am a slave (*with dat. of pers.*).

Servius, -i, 2 *m.,* Servius.

servo, 1 *v. a.,* I keep, preserve.

servus, -i, 2 *m.,* a slave.

sevērus, -a, -um, *adj.,* severe, serious, stern, sober.

sex, *num. adj.,* six.

sexāgintā, *num. adj.,* sixty.

sextus, -a, -um, *ord. adj.,* sixth.

sextus decimus, *ord. adj.,* six-teenth.

sī, *conj.,* if.

Sibyllīnus, -a, -um, *adj.,* Sibyl-line.

sīc, *adv.,* thus, so.

sīcārius, -i, 2 *m.,* an assassin.

Sicilia, -ae, 1 *f.,* Sicily.

significo, 1 *v. a.,* I make known, declare.

signum, -i, 2 *n.,* a sign, statue.

silva, -ae, 1 *f.,* a wood.

simplicitas, -ātis, 3 *f.,* simplicity.

simul, *adv.,* together, at the same time.

sine, *prep. with abl.,* without.

sinistra, -ae, 1 *f.,* left-hand.

sitis, -is, 3 *f.,* thirst.

societas, -ātis, 3 *f.,* alliance, share.

socius, -ii, 2 *m.,* an ally.

sōl, sōlis, 3 *m.,* the sun.

solea, -ae, 1 *f.,* a slipper, sandal (*worn by men only in the house*).

sollicito, 1 *v. a.,* I tempt, bribe.

sollicitūdo, -inis, 3 *f.,* anxiety, care.

Solōn, -ōnis, 3 *m.,* Solon.

sōlum, *adv.,* only.

solum, -i, 2 *n.,* the ground, floor, pavement.

sōlus, -a, -um, *adj.,* only, alone.

somnus, -i, 2 *m.,* sleep.

spatium, -ii, 2 *n.,* space, room.

speciēs, -ēi, 5 *f.,* form, shape, species.

spectāculum, -i, 2 *n.,* show, spectacle.

specto, 1 *v. a.,* I look at, see, weigh, examine.

spēlunca, -ae, 1 *f.,* a cave.

spēro, 1 *v. a.,* I hope.

spēs, spei, 5 *f.,* hope.

splendidus, -a, -um, *adj.,* splendid, brilliant.

stadium, -ii, 2 *n.,* a race-course.

statim, *adv.,* immediately.

statua, -ae, 1 *f.,* a statue, image.

steti, *perf. of* sto.

sto, stāre, steti, statum, 1 *v. n.*, I stand; iudicio sto, I stand by my judgment *or* opinion.

Stōicus, -i, 2 *m.*, a Stoic philosopher.

strēnuus, -a, -um, *adj.*, energetic, vigorous.

strepitus, -ūs, 4 *m.*, noise, din.

struo, -ere, -xi, -ctum, 3 *v. a.*, I build, prepare.

studeo, 2 *v. n.*, I desire, wish.

studium, -ii, 2 *n.*, study, pursuit, desire; *in plur.*, studies.

stultus, -a, -um, *adj.*, foolish.

subitō, *adv.*, suddenly.

subsidium, -i, 2 *n.*, help, aid.

sum, esse, fui, *v. n.*, I am.

summus, -a, -um, *adj.*, highest; summus mons, the top of the mountain.

superbia, -ae, 1 *f.*, pride.

superbus, -a, -um, *adj.*, proud.

superior, -us, *comp. adj.*, superior, stronger.

supero, 1 *v. a.*, I overcome, vanquish.

super-sum, -esse, -fui, *v. n.*, I remain, survive.

supplicium, -i, 2 *n.*, punishment.

surgo, -ere, sur-rexi, surrectum, 3 *v. n.*, I rise.

suus, -a, -um, *poss. and reflex. pron.*, his, her, its, their.

tabula, -ae, 1 *f.*, a painted tablet, picture.

tabulīnum, -i, 2 *n.*, a study, office.

taceo, 2 *v. n.*, I am silent.

tam, *adv.*, so, so much.

tamen, *conj.*, however, nevertheless.

tandem, *adv.*, at last, at length.

tardus, -a, -um, *adj.*, slow.

Tarquinius, -i, 2 *m.*, Tarquinius.

Tartarus, -i, 2 *m.*, Tartarus.

tectum, -i, 2 *m.*, roof, house.

tego, -ere, -xi, -ctum, 3 *v. a.*, I cover, hide, protect.

tegumentum, -i, 2 *n.*, a covering.

tēlum, -i, 2 *n.*, a weapon, missile.

templum, -i, 2 *n.*, a temple.

tempus, -oris, 3 *n.*, time, season.

tenĕbrae, -ārum, 1 *f. pl.*, darkness.

teneo, -ēre, tenui, tentum, 2 *v. a.*, I hold, keep.

tener, -era, -erum, *adj.*, tender.

tento, 1 *v. a.*, I attempt, tempt.

tergum, -i, 2 *n.*, the back, rear.

termino, 1 *v. a.*, I limit, define, determine.

terra, -ae, 1 *f.*, land, earth.

terreo, 2 *v. a.*, I frighten.

terribilis, -e, *adj.*, terrible.

terror, -ōris, 3 *m.*, terror, fright.

tertiō, *adv.*, thirdly.

tertius, -a, -um, *ord. adj.*, third.

Teutoni, -ōrum, 2 *m. pl.*, the Teutons.

Thalēs, -is *and* -lētis, 3 *m.*, Thales.

thermae, -arum, 1 *f. pl.*, baths.

timeo, 2 *v. n.*, I fear.

timor, -ōris, 3 *m.*, fear.

titulus, -i, 2 *m.*, an inscription.

tollo, -ere, sustuli, sublātum, 3 *v. a.*, I take away.

tot, *num. adj. indecl.*, so many.

tōtus, -a, -um (*gen.* tōtīus), *adj.*, all, the whole.

tracto, 1 *v. a.*, I treat, handle, deal with.

trādo, -ere, trādidī, trāditum, 3 *v.a.*, I hand over, deliver.

trāicio, -ere, -iēci, -iectum, 3 *v. a.*, I cause to cross, lead across, transport.

tranquillus, -a, -um, *adj.*, calm.

trans-porto, 1 *v. a.*, I carry across.

trecenti, -ae, -a, *num. adj.*, three hundred.

trēs, tria, *num. adj.*, three.

triclīnium, -i, 2 *n.*, a dining-couch (*running round three sides of table*); a dining-room.

trigintā, *num. adj.*, thirty.

tristis, -e, *adj.*, sad, gloomy.

triumphus, -i, 2 *m.*, a triumph, triumphal procession.

Trōia, -ae, 1 *f.*, Troy.

Trōiānus, -a, -um, *adj.*, Trojan.

trucīdo, 1 *v. a.*, I slay, butcher.

tū, *2nd pers. pron.*, thou, you.

Tullius, -i, 2 *m.*, Tullius.

Tullus, -i, 2 *m.*, Tullus.

tum, *adv.*, then, at that time.

turbulentus, -a, -um, *adj.*, noisy, turbulent.

turpis, -e, *adj.*, disgraceful, base.

turris, -is, 3 *f.*, a tower, turret.

tūtēla, -ae, 1 *f.*, protection, guard.

tūtus, -a, -um, *adj.*, safe, protected.

tuus, -a, -um, *poss. pron.*, thy, your.

ubī, *adv.*, where? when, in which, where.

Ulixes, -is, 3 *m.*, Ulysses.

ultimus, -a, -um, *sup. adj.*, furthest, furthest part of

ūnā, *adv.*, together with.

unde, *adv.*, whence?

undique, *adv.*, on all sides, from all parts.

ūnus, -a, -um, *num. adj.*, one, the only.

urbs, urbis, 3 *f.*, a city.

ut, *conj.*, as, when.

ūtilis, -e, *adj.*, useful, expedient

uxor, -ōris, 3 *f.*, a wife.

valdē, *adv.*, very greatly, much

valē, farewell !

valeo, 2 *v. n.*, I am strong, in good health.

validus, -a, -um, *adj.*, strong.

vallum, -i, 2 *n.*, a rampart.

vānus, -a, -um, *adj.*, useless, vain.

vasto, 1 *v.a.*, I lay waste, ravage.

veho, -ere, vexi, vectum, 3 *v. a.*, I carry ; equo vehor, I ride *or* drive.

vel, *conj.*, or ; vel . . . vel, either . . . or (*that is, take your choice*).

vene_or,-āri,-ātus sum, 1 *v. dep.*, I revere, reverence, honour.

venia, -ae, 1 *f.*, pardon, permission, leave.

venio, -īre, vēni, ventum, 4 *v.a.*, I come.

ventus, -i, 2 *m.*, wind.

vēr, vēris, 3 *n.*, spring.

verbum, -i, 2 *n.*, a word ; verba facio, I speak, plead.

Vergilius, -i, 2 *m.*, Vergil.

versor,-āri,-ātus sum, 1 *v. pass.*, I am engaged in.

vērus, -a, -um, *adj.*, true.

vester, -tra, -trum, *poss. adj.*,
　　your.
vestibulum, -i, 2 *n.*, entrance-
　　court, hall.
vestio, 4 *v. a.*, I clothe, dress.
vetulus, -a, -um, *adj.*, old ;
　　hence vetula, -ae, 1 *f.*,
　　a little old woman.
vexo, 1 *v. a.*, I annoy, harass.
via, -ae, 1 *f.*, way, road, journey.
victor, -ōris, 3 *m.*, winner, con-
　　queror.
victōria, -ae, 1 *f.*, victory.
victus, -ūs, 4 *m.*, way of living.
vīcus, -i, 2 *m.*, a village.
video, -ēre, vīdi, vīsum, 2 *v. a.*,
　　I see.
vigintī, *num. adj.*, twenty.
villa, -ae, 1 *f.*, a country-house,
　　farm.
vincio, -īre, vinxi, vinctum,
　　4 *v. a.*, I bind.
vinco, -ere, vīci, victum, 3 *v. a.*,
　　I conquer.
vīnum, -i, 2 *n.*, wine.
vir, viri, 2 *m.*, a man, hero,
　　husband.

virtūs, -ūtis, 3 *f.*, virtue, valour,
　　courage.
vīso, -ere, vīsi, vīsum, 3 *v. a.*,
　　I go to see, visit.
vīta, -ae, 1 *f.*, life.
vitium, -ii, 2 *n.*, vice.
vīto, 1 *v. a.*, I avoid.
vitupero, 1 *v. a.*, I blame, cen-
　　sure.
vīvo, -ere, vixi, victum, 3 *v. n.*,
　　I live.
vix, *adv.*, hardly, scarcely.
voco, 1 *v. a.*, I call.
volo, velle, volui, *v. irreg. a.*
　　and n., I wish, am willing,
　　want.
voluntas, -ātis, 3 *f.*, wish,
　　will.
voluptas, -ātis, 3 *f.*, pleasure.
vulnero, 1 *v. a.*, I wound.
vultus, -ūs, 4 *m.*, face, counte-
　　nance.

Zēno, -ōnis, 3 *m.*, Zeno.

ENGLISH-LATIN INDEX

—•—

able (I am), possum, posse, potui, *v. irreg.*

about, dē, *prep. (with abl.).*

absent (I am), absum, abesse, āfui, *v. n.*

Achilles, Achilles, -is, 3 *m.*

according to, ad, *prep. (with acc.).*

account (on account of), ob, *prep. (with acc.).*

address (I), verba facio.

admire (I), admīror, -āri, -ātus sum, 1 *v. dep.*

adorn (I), orno, 1 *v. a.*

adversary (an), adversārius, -i, 2 *m.* ; hostis, -is, 3 *m.*

adverse, adversus, -a, -um, *adj.*

advice, consilium, -i, 2 *n.*

advise (I), moneo, -ēre, -ui, -itum, 2 *v. a.*

affair, negōtium, -i, 2 *n.* ; rēs, reī, 5 *f.*

Africa, Africa, -ae, 1 *f.*

after, post, *prep. (with acc.);* posteā, *adv.* ; postquam, *conj.*

afterwards, posteā, *adv.*

again, iterum *or* rursus, *adv.*

against, contrā, *prep. (with acc.).*

aid, auxilium, -i, 2 *n.*

Alexander, Alexander, -dri, 2 *m.*

all, all sorts of, omnis, -e, *adj.*

alone, sōlus, -a, -um, *or* ūnus, -a, -um, *adj.* ; sōlum *or* modo, *adv.*

Alps, Alpes, Alpium, 3 *f. pl.*

already, iam, *adv.*

also, etiam *or* quoque, *adv.*

altar, āra, -ae, 1 *f.*

always, semper, *adv.*

ambassador, lēgātus, -i, 2 *m.*

among, inter *or* apud, *prep. (with acc.).*

ample, amplus, -a, -um, *adj.*

ancient, antīquus, -a, -um, *adj.*

and, et *or* -que, *conj. (the latter always joined to the end of the second word).*

and not, neque *or* nec, *conj.* (neque *before vowels*).

and now, iamque, *conj.*

and so, itaque, *conj.*

anger, īra, -ae, 1 *f.*

another, alius, -a, -ud, *adj.*

Apollo, Apollo, -inis, 3 *m.*

appease (I), plāco, 1 *v. a.*

appoint (I), creo, 1 *v. a.*, *or* nōmino, 1 *v. a.*

approach (to a place), aditus, -ūs, 4 *m.*; (of a person) adventus, -ūs, 4 *m.*

approach (I), appropinquo, 1 *v. n.* (*with* ad *and acc.*).

arms, arma, -ōrum, 2 *n. pl.*; arma capio, I take up arms.

army, exercitus, -ūs, 4 *m.*

arouse (I), excito, 1 *v. a.*

arrival, adventus, -ūs, 4 *m.*

arrive (I), adsum, -esse, -fui, *v. n.*

art, ars, artis, 3 *f.*

Asia, Ăsia, -ae, 1 *f.*

ask (I), rogo (*with double acc.*), *or* postulo (*with prep.* ā *and abl. of person*), 1 *v. a.*

assassin, sīcārius, -i, 2 *m.*

at, ad *and* apud (near), *prep.* (*with acc.*); in (in *or* on), *prep.* (*with abl.*).

at a great price, magno pretio.

at first, prīmō, *adv.*

at home, domī.

at last *or* **at length**, tandem, *adv.*

at once, statim, *adv.*

Athenians, Athēnienses, -ium, 3 *m. pl.*

attack, impetus, -ūs, 4 *m.*

attack (I), oppugno, 1 *v. a.*

attempt (I), cōnor, -āri, -ātus sum, 1 *v. dep.*

attendant, satelles, -itis, 3 *m.*; minister, -tri, 2 *m.*

Augustus, Augustus, -i, 2 *m.*

Australia, Austrālia, -ae, 1 *f.*

author, scriptor, -ōris, 3 *m.*

authority, auctōritas, -ātis, 3 *f.*

autumn, auctumnus, -i, 2 *m.*

avarice, avāritia, -ae, 1 *f.*

avoid (I), vīto, 1 *v. a.*

await (I), exspecto, 1 *v. a.*

awake (I), excito, 1 *v. a.*, *or* excio, 4 *v. a.*

away from, ā *or* ab, *prep.* (*with abl.*).

bad, malus, -a, -um, *adj.*

Baiae, Baiae, -ārum, 1 *f. pl.*

barbarian, barbarus, -a, -um, *adj.*; barbarus, -i, 2 *m.*

base, turpis, -e, *adj.*

battle, pugna, -ae, 1 *f.*, *or* proelium, -i, 2 *n.*

beautiful, pulcher, -chra, -chrum, *adj.*

beauty, pulchritūdo, -dinis, 3 *f.*, *or* forma, -ae, 1 *f.*

because, quia *or* quod, *conj.*

before, ante, *prep.* (*with acc.*); anteā, *adv.*; antequam, *conj.*

behold, ecce! *interj.* (*with nom.*).

behold (I), specto, 1 *v. a.*, *or* conspicio, -ere, -spexi, -spectum, 3 *v. a.*

bend (I), flecto, -ere, flexi, flexum, 3 *v. a.*

besiege (I), oppugno, 1 *v. a.*, *or* obsideo, -ere, -sēdi, -sessum, 2 *v. a.*

best, optimus, -a, -um, *adj.*

betake (I), recipio, -ere, -cēpi, -ceptum, 3 *v. a.* (*with acc. of pers. pron.*, mē, tē, &c.).

better, melior, -us, *adj.*

between, inter, *prep.* (*with acc.*).

beware (I), caveo, -ēre, cāvi, cautum, 2 *v. a.*

blame, culpa, -ae, 1 *f.*

blame (I), culpo, 1 *v. a.*

blind, caecus, -a, -um, *adj.*

blind (I), caeco, I *v. a.*

blot out (I), dēleo, -ēre, -ēvi, -ētum, 2 *v. a.*

body, corpus, -poris, 3 *n.*

boldness, audācia, -ae, I *f.*

book, liber, -bri, 2 *m.*

book-case, pluteus, -i, 2 *m.*

both . . . and, et . . . et, *conj.*

bother (I), ango, -ere, anxi, anctum, 3 *v. a.*

boy, puer, pueri, 2 *m.*

brave, fortis, -e, *adj.*

bring (I), porto, I *v. a.*

bring about (I), commoveo, -ēre, -mōvi, -mōtum, 2 *v.a.*

Britons (the), Britanni, -ōrum, 2 *m. pl.*

broad, lātus, -a, -um, *adj.*

brother, frāter, -tris, 3 *m.*

build (I), aedifico, I *v. a.*

building, aedificium, -i, 2 *n.*

burden, onus, -eris, 3 *n.*

burn (I), cremo, I *v. a.*

bust, imāgo, -ginis, 3 *f.*

but, sed, *conj.*, *or* autem, *conj.* (autem *cannot stand first*) ; but not, neque, *conj.*

by, ā *or* ab (*before a vowel*) ; *only after a passive verb before the name of a person.*

Caesar, Caesar, -aris, 3 *m.*

call (I), appello, I *v. a.* ; nōmino, I *v.a.* ; voco, I *v.a.*

call together (I), convoco, I *v.a.*

calm (I), lēnio, 4 *v. a.*

Camillus, Camillus, -i, 2 *m.*

camp, castra, -ōrum, 2 *n. pl.*

can (I), possum, posse, potui, *v. n.*

Cannae (of), Cannensis, -e, *adj.*

capture (I), capio, -ere, cēp captum, 3 *v. a.*

care, cūra, -ae, I *f.* ; with care cum cūrā ; *pred. dat.*, cūrae an object of care.

care (I take), caveo, -ēre, cāvi cautum, 2 *v. n.*

carry out *or* on (I), gero, -ere gessi, gestum, 3 *v. a.*

Carthage, Carthāgo, -ginis 3 *f.*

Carthaginian, Pūnicus, -a -um, *adj.*

Carthaginians (the), Poeni -ōrum, 2 *m. pl.*

Cassivellaunus, Cassivellaunus, -i, 2 *m.*

cause, causa, -ae, I *f.*

cavalry, equites, -um, 3 *m. pl.*

cave, spēlunca, -ae, I *f.*

celebrate (I), celebro, I *v. a.*

celebrated, praeclārus, -a, -um, *adj.*

Cerberus, Cerberus, -i, 2 *m.*

certain, certus, -a, -um, *adj.*

change (I), mūto, I *v. a.*

chariot, currus, -ūs, 4 *m.* ; *or* quādrīgae, -ārum, I *f. pl.*

cherish (I), dīligo, -ere, -lexi, -lectum, 3 *v. a.*

chestnut, castanea, -ae, I *f.*

choose (I), dēligo, -ere, -lēgi, -lectum, 3 *v. a.*

citizen, cīvis, -is, 3 *m. and f.*

city, urbs, urbis, 3 *f.*

Clitus, Clītus, -i, 2 *m.*

cloak, lacerna, -ae, I *f.*

close (I), claudo, -ere, -si, -sum, 3 *v. a.*

clothe (I), vestio, 4 *v. a.*

cognomen, cognōmen, -minis, 3 *n.*

cold, frīgus, -goris, 3 *n.*

cold, frīgidus, -a, -um, *adj.*

colony, colōnia, -ae, 1 *f.*

column, columna, -ae, 1 *f.*

come (I), venio, -īre, vēni, ventum, 4 *v. n.* ; adsum, -esse, -fui, *v. n.* ; come hither! hūc ades!

commencement, exordium, -i, 2 *n.*

companion, comes, -itis, 3 m.

compare (I), comparo, 1 *v. a.*

complete (I), compleo, -ēre, -ēvi, -ētum, 2 *v. a.*

conceal (I), cēlo, 1 *v. a.*

condemn (I), damno, 1 *v. a.*

confidence, fidēs, -eī, 5 *f.* ; I place confidence in, fidem habeo (*with dat. of person*).

conquer (I), vinco, -ere, vīci, victum, 3 *v. a.*

conqueror, victor, -ōris, 3 *m.*

console, sōlor, -āri, -ātus sum, 1 *v. dep.*

consul, consul, -ulis, 3 *m.*

contemplate (I), contemplor, -āri, -ātus sum, 1 *v. dep.*

content, contentus, -a, -um, *adj.* (*with abl.*).

conversation, sermo, -ōnis, 3 *m.*

copy (I), itero, 1 *v. a.*

corn, frūmentum, -i, 2 *n.*

couch, lectus, -i, 2 *m.*

counsel, consilium, -i, 2 *n.*

country, patria, -ae, 1 *f.* ; *opp. to town,* rūs, rūris, 3 *n.*

country-house, villa, -ae, 1 *f.*

courage, virtūs, -ūtis, 3 *f.*

course, cursus, -ūs, 4 *m.*

court, peristȳlium, -i, 2 *n.*

covetous, cupidus, -a, -um, *adj.* (*with gen.*).

crime, scelus, -eris, 3 *n.*

cross over (I), mīgro, 1 *v. a.*

crowded, celeber, -ēbris, -ēbre, *adj.*

crush (I), opprimo, -ere, -pres-si, -pressum, 3 *v. a.*

cry, clāmor, -ōris, 3 *m.*

cry out (I), clāmo, 1 *v. n.*

Cumae, Cūmae, -ārum, 1 *f. pl.*

cunning, dolus, -i, 2 *m.*

custom, mōs, mōris, 3 *m.*

daily, quotīdiē, *adv.*

danger, perīculum, -i, 2 *n.*

dangerous, perīculōsus, -a, -um, *adj.*

day, diēs, diēī, 5 *m.*

day (to-), hodiē, *adv.*

dead, mortuus, -a, -um, *adj.* ; the dead, mortui, -ōrum, 2 *m. pl.*

dear, cārus, -a, -um, *adj.*

death, mors, mortis, 3 *f.* ; I condemn to death, capitis damno.

deceive (I), dēcipio, -ere, -cēpi, -ceptum, 3 *v. a.*

December, December, -bris, 3 *m.*

declare (I), indīco, -ere, -xi, -ctum, 3 *v. a.* ; I declare war on, bellum indīco (*with dat. of pers.*).

deed, factum, -i, 2 *n.* ; rēs, reī, 5 *f.*

defeat (I), supero, 1 *v. a.* ; vinco, -ere, vīci, victum, 3 *v. a.*

delay, mora, -ae, 1 *f.*

delight (I), dēlecto, 1 *v. a.*

demand (I), postulo, 1 *v. a.* (*with prep.* ā *or* ab *and* abl. *of pers.*).

depart (I), abeo, -īre, -ii, -itum, *v. n.*

design, consilium, -i, 2 *n.*

desire (I), opto, 1 *v.a.* ; studeo, 2 *v. n.*; cupio, -ere, -īvi, -ītum, 3 *v. a.*

dessert, mensa secunda.

destroy (I), dēleo, -ēre, -ēvi, -ētum, 2 *v. a.*

destructive, perniciōsus, -a, -um, *adj.*

deter (I), dēterreo, 2 *v. a.* (*with prep.* ā *or* ab *and abl. of thing*).

devise (I), fingo, -ere, finxi, fictum, 3 *v. a.*

Diana, Diāna, -ae, 1 *f.*

dictator, dictātor, -ōris, 3 *m.*

dictatorship, dictātūra, -ae, 1 *f.*

die (I), morior, mori, mortuus sum, 3 *v. dep.*

difficult, difficilis, -e, *adj.*

difficulty (with), aegrē, *adv.*

Diogenes, Diogenes, -is, 3 *m.*

direct (I), dīrigo, -ere, -rexi, -rectum, 3 *v.a.*

directions (in all), undique, *adv.*

disagreeable, molestus, -a, -um, *adj.*

disaster, incommodum, -i, 2 *n.*; clādes, -is, 3 *f.*

disgrace, dēdecus, -oris, 3 *n.*; *pred. dat.,* dēdecori, an object of disgrace.

disgraceful, turpis, -e, *adj.*

distant (I am), absum, abesse, āfui, *v. n.* (*with prep.* ab, *from*).

distinguished, praeclārus, -a, -um, *adj.*; praestans, -antis, *adj.*

distress (I), sollicito, 1 *v. a.*

disturb (I), perturbo, 1 *v. a.*

do (I), ago, -ere, ēgi, actum, 3 *v. a.*; facio, -ere, fēci factum, 3 *v. a.*

dog, canis, -is, 3 *m.*

door, porta, -ae, 1 *f.* ; ostium -i, 2 *n.*

draw away (I), abstraho, -ere -xi, -ctum, 3 *v. a.* (*with prep.* ā *or* ab).

drive (I), fugo, 1 *v. a.* ; pello, -ere, pepuli, pulsum, 3 *v. a.*

due (I am), dēbeor, -ēri, dēbitus sum, 2 *v. pass.*

due, dēbitus, -a, -um, *adj.*

during, *expressed by acc. of duration.*

duty, *it is the duty of,* est, *with gen. of person.*

eager, cupidus, -a, -um, *adj.* (*with gen.*).

easily, facile, *adv.*

easy, facilis, -e, *adj.*

educate (I), ēduco, 1 *v. a.*

Egypt, Aegyptus, -i, 2 *f.*

Egyptian, Aegyptius, -a, -um, *adj.*

eighth, octāvus, -a, -um, *adj.*

elect (I), creo, 1 *v. a.* ; ēligo, -ere, -lēgi, -lectum, 3 *v. a.*

element, elementum, -i, 2 *n.*

elementary (school), (lūdus) litterārius, -a, -um, *adj.*

emperor, imperātor, -ōris, 3 *m.*

end, fīnis, -is, 3 *m.*

enemy, hostis, -is, 3 *m.* (public); inimīcus, -i, 2 *m.* (private).

enough, satis, *indecl. adj. and adv.*

enter (I), intro, 1 *v. a. and n.* ; ineo, -īre, -ii, -itum, *v. n.* (*with* in *and acc.*).

entrance, aditus, -ūs, 4 *m.*

envy, invidia, -ae, 1 *f.*

err (I), erro, 1 *v. n.*

escape (I), fugio, -ere, fūgi, fugitum, 3 *v. n.*

esteem (I), dīligo, -ere, -lexi, -lectum, 3 *v. a.*

ever, semper, *adv.* (always); unquam, *adv.* (at any time).

every, omnis, -e, *adj.* ; everything, omnia, *n. pl.*

everywhere, undique, *adv.*

example, exemplum, -i, 2 *n.*

excellent, praeclārus, -a, -um, *adj.*; praestans, -antis, *adj.*

except, nisi, *conj.*

excite, excito, 1 *v. a.*

exercise (I), exerceo, 2 *v. a.*

exhort (I), hortor, -āri, -ātus sum, 1 *v. dep.*

expect (I), exspecto, 1 *v. a.*

expedient, ūtilis, -e, *adj.*

explain (I), explico, 1 *v. a.*

eye, oculus, -i, 2 *m.*

Fabricius, Fābricius, -i, 2 *m.*

fail (I), dēficio, -ere, -fēci, -fectum, 3 *v. n.*

fair, aequus, -a, -um, *adj.*

faithful, fīdus, -a, -um, *adj.*

fame, fāma, -ae, 1 *f.* ; glōria, -ae, 1 *f.*

famous, praeclārus, -a, -um, *adj.*

far off, procul, *adv.*

farewell, valē ! *pl.* valēte !

farmer, āgricola, -ae, 1 *m.*

father, pater, pătris, 3 *m.*

favourable, secundus, -a, -um, *adj.*; propitius, -a, -um, *adj.*

fear, timor, -ōris, 3 *m.*; through fear, timōre.

fear (I), timeo, 2 *v. a.* ; vereor, -ēri, veritus sum, 2 *v. dep.*

February, Februārius, -i, 2 *m.*

few, paucus, -a, -um, *adj.*

field, ager, ăgri, 2 *m.*

fierce, saevus, -a, -um, *adj.*

fifteen, quindecim, *num. adj.*

fifty, quinquāgintā, *num. adj.*

fight (I), pugno, 1 *v. n.*

fight, pugna, -ae, 1 *f.* ; proelium, -i, 2 *n.*

figure, figūra, -ae, 1 *f.*

fill(I), compleo, -ēre, -ēvi, -ētum, 2 *v. a.*, *and* I fill up, impleo, -ēre, -ēvi, -ētum, 2 *v.a.*

filled with, plēnus, -a, -um, *adj.* (*with abl. or gen.*).

final, ultimus, -a, -um, *adj.*

finish, fīnio, 4 *v. a.*

fire, ignis, -is, 3 *m.*

firm, firmus, -a, -um, *adj.* ; constans, -antis, *adj.*

first, prīmus, -a, -um, *ord. adj.* ; at first, prīmō, *adv.*

five, quinque, *num. adj.*

five hundred, quingenti, -ae, -a, *num. adj.*

flee (I), fugio, -ere, fūgi, fugitum, 3 *v. n.*

fleet, classis, -is, 3 *f.*

flight, fuga, -ae, 1 *f.*

floor, solum, -i, 2 *n.*

fond, cupidus, -a, -um, *adj.* (*with gen.*).

foolish, stultus, -a, -um, *adj.*

foot, pēs, pedis, ~~adj~~ — 𝓃𝓇 𝓊 𝓃

foot-soldier, pedes, peditis, 3 *m.*

for (because), nam *or* enim, *conj.* (enim *cannot stand first*).

for (on behalf of), prō, *prep.* (*with abl.*).

for (on account of), ob, *prep.*, *and* propter, *prep.* (*with acc.*).

for a long time, diū, *adv.*

forces, cōpiae, -ārum, 1 *f. pl.*

form (I), formo, 1 *v. a.*; I form (a friendship), iungo, -ere, iunxi, iunctum, 3 *v. a.*

former, ille, illa, illud, *pron.* (*opp. to* hic, the latter).

formerly, ōlim, *adv.*

fortifications, moenia, -ium, 3 *n. pl.*

fortify (I), mūnio, 4 *v. a.*

fortune, fortūna, -ae, 1 *f.*

forty, quādrāginta, *num. adj.*

four, quattuor, *num. adj.*

four hundred, quādringenti, -ae, -a, *num. adj.*

fraud, fraus, fraudis, 3 *f.*

free (I), lībero, 1 *v. a.* (*with abl. of thing freed from*).

friend, amīcus, -i, 2 *m.*

friendship, amīcitia, -ae, 1 *f.*

frighten (I), terreo, 2 *v. a.*

from, ā *or* ab (*before vowels*), *prep.* (*with abl.*); ē *or* ex (*out of*); dē (*down from*).

from all sides, undique, *adv.*

frugality, frūgālitas, -ātis, 3 *f.*

fruit, fructus, -ūs, 4 *m.*

full, plēnus, -a, -um, *adj.* (*with gen. or abl.*).

gain (I), reporto, 1 *v. a.* (*with ā or ab of person over whom victory is gained*).

game, lūsus, -ūs, 4 *m.*; games, lūdi, -ōrum, 2 *m. pl.*

garden, hortus, -i, 2 *m.*

Gaul, Gallia, -ae, 1 *f.*

Gauls, Galli, -ōrum, 2 *m. pl.*

gave (I), dedi.

general, dux, ducis, 3 *m.*, *or* imperātor, -ōris, 3 *m.*

get ready (I), paro, 1 *v. a.*, expedio, 4 *v. a.*

gift, dōnum, -i, 2 *n.*, *or* mūnu -eris, 3 *n.*

give (I), do, dare, dedi, datur 1 *v. a.*; I give thank grātias ago.

glad (I am), gaudeo, -ēre, gāv sus sum, 2 *v. n.* (*with con quod, because or that*).

glory, glōria, -ae, 1 *f.*

go (I), eo, īre, īvi *or* ii, itun *v. n.*

go away (I), abeo, -īre, -i -itum, *v. n.*

go on board (I), (navem) cor scendo, -ere, -di, -sum 3 *v. a.*

go forth (I), prōdeo, -īre, -ii -itum, 3 *v. n.*

go out (I), exeo, -īre, -ii, -itum *v. n.* (*with prep.* ex).

goblet, pōculum, -i, 2 *n.*

god, deus, dei, 2 *m.*

goddess, dea, deae, 1 *f.*

good, bonus, -a, -um, *adj.*

good-day, salvē! *pl.* salvēte!

goodness, probitas, -ātis, 3 *f.*

Graces, Grātiae, -ārum, 1 *f. pl.*

grandfather, avus, -i, 2 *m.*

grant (I), do, dare, dedi, datum, 1 *v. a.*

grateful, grātus, -a, -um, *adj.*; I am grateful, grātiam habeo.

great, magnus, -a, -um, *adj.*

greater, māior, -us, *comp. adj.*

greatest, maximus, -a, -um, *sup. adj.*

Greece, Graecia, -ae, 1 *f.*

Greek, Graecus, -a, -um, *adj.*

grief, dolor, -ōris, 3 *m.*

grieve (I), doleo, 2 *v. n.* (*with conj.* quod, because).

guard, custōs, -ōdis, 3 *m.*

guard (I), custōdio, 4 *v. a.*

guide, dux, ducis, 3 *f.*

gymnasium, gymnasium, -i, 2 *n.*

hall, vestibulum, -i, 2 *n.* (entrance); ātrium, -i, 2 *n.* (principal room).

hand, manus, -ūs, 4 *f.*

handle (I), tracto, 1 *v. a.*

hands (in hands of), penes, *prep.* (*with acc.*).

Hannibal, Hannibal, -alis, 3 *m.*

happy, beātus, -a, -um, *adj.*

harbour, portus, -ūs, 4 *m.*

hard, dūrus, -a, -um, *adj.*; severus, -a, -um, *adj.*

hasten (I), propero, 1 *v. n.*; mātūro, 1 *v. a.*; I hasten flight, fugam maturo.

have (I), habeo, 2 *v. a.*

he, is, *gen.* ēius, *dem. pron.*

head, caput, -itis, 3 *n.*

hear (I), audio, 4 *v. a.*

heavily, graviter, *adv.*

heavy, gravis, -e, *adj.*

help, auxilium, -i, 2 *n.*

here, hic, *adv.*

here is, ecce ! *adv.* (*with nom.*).

here (I am), adsum, -esse, -fui, *v. n.*

hero, vir, viri, 2 *m.*

herself, sē, *gen.* suī, *reflex. pron.*

herself (she), ipsa, *pron.*

high, altus, -a, -um, *adj.*

highly (I value highly), magni; more highly, plūris, *gen. of price.*

hill, mons, montis, 3 *m.*

him, *oblique cases of* is, *pron.*

himself, sē, *gen.* suī, *reflex. pron.*

himself (he), ipse, *pron.*

hinder (I), impedio, 4 *v. a.* (*with prep.* ā *or* ab, from).

hindrance, impedīmentum, -i, 2 *n.*

his (his own), suus, -a, -um, *reflex. pron.*; his, ēius, *not reflex.*

hither, hūc, *adv.*

hold (I), teneo, -ēre, tenui, tentum, 2 *v. a.*

hold back (I), retineo, -ēre, -ui, -tentum, 2 *v. a.*

hold out (I), ostendo, -ere, -di, -sum *and* -tum, 3 *v. a.*

holy, sanctus, -a, -um, *adj.*

home, domus, -ūs, 4 *f.*

home at, domī, *locative.*

Homer, Homērus, -i, 2 *m.*

honest, honestus, -a, -um, *adj.*

honesty, honestas, -ātis, 3 *f.*

honour, honor, -ōris, 3 *m.*; (honesty), honestas, -ātis, 3 *f.*

honour (I), veneror, -āri, -ātus sum, 1 *v. dep.*

honourable, honestus, -a, -um, *adj.*

hope, spes, spei, 5 *f.*

Horatius, Horātius, -i, 2 *m.*

horse, equus, -i, 2 *m.*

horse-soldier, eques, -itis, 3 *m.*

hostile, inimīcus, -a, -um, *adj.*

house, domus, -ūs, 4 *f.* (*abl. sing.* domō, *acc. plur.* domōs).

how, quam, *adv.*

how ? quōmodo ? *adv.*

however, tamen, *adv.* (*cannot stand first*).

how many ? quot ? *indecl. adj.*

humble, humilis, -e, *adj.*

I, ego, 1 *pers. pron.*; it is I, ego sum.

if, sī, *conj.*

ill, male, *adv.*

illustrious, praeclārus, -a, -um, *adj.*

image, imāgo, -inis, 3 *f.*

immediately, statim, *adv.*

immense, ingens, -entis, *adv.*

in, in, *prep.* (*with abl.*).

in all directions, passim; undique, *adv.*

in hands of, penes, *prep.* (*with acc.*).

in vain, frustrā, *adv.*

increase (I), augeo, -ēre, auxi, auctum, 2 *v. a.*

inclined, facilis, -e, *adj.* (*often with prep.* ad, to).

infantry, pedites, -um, 3 *m. pl.*

inhabitant, incola, -ae, 1 *m. and f.*

injury, iniūria, -ae, 1 *f.*

innocent, innocens, -entis, *adj.*

insult, contumēlia, -ae, 1 *f.*; iniūria, -ae, 1 *f.*

integrity, integritas, -ātis, 3 *f.*

into, in, *prep.* (*with acc.*).

island, insula, -ae, 1 *f.*

it, is, ea, id, *dem. pron.*; it is I, ego sum.

Italy, Ītalia, -ae, 1 *f.*

Janus, Iānus, -i, 2 *m.*

join (I), iungo, -ere, iunxi, iunctum, 3 *v. a.*; they join themselves to, sē iungunt (*with dat. of pers.*).

journey, iter, itineris, 3 *n.*; I hasten my journey, iter mātūro.

joy, gaudium, -i, 2 *n.*

judge, iūdex, iūdicis, 3 *m.*

Julius, Iūlius, -i, 2 *m.*

Jupiter, Iuppiter, Iovis, 3 *m.*

just, modo; (lately) nūper, *adv*

keep (I), servo, 1 *v. a.* (I preserve); teneo, -ēre, tenui, tentum, 2 *v. a.* (I detain, hold): I keep in memory, memoriā teneo; I keep in camp, in castris habeo *or* teneo.

kill (I), neco, 1 *v. a.*; interficio, -ere, -fēci, -fectum, 3 *v. a.*

kind, benignus, -a, -um, *adj.*

kindness, benignitas, -ātis, 3 *f.*

king, rex, rēgis, 3 *m.*

kingdom, imperium, -i, 2 *n.*, *or* regnum, -i, 2 *n.*

knee, genū, -ūs, 4 *n.*

knock *or* knock at (I), pulso, 1 *v. a.*

know (I), scio, 4 *v. a.*

known, nōtus, -a, -um, *adj.*

labour, labor, -ōris, 3 *m.*

laden, onerātus, -a, -um, *adj.*

land, terra, -ae, 1 *f.*, *or* ager, āgri, 2 *m.*

land, *adj.*, pedestris, -e.

large, magnus, -a, -um, *adj.*

last, ultimus, -a, -um, *adj.*

last (at), tandem, *adv.*

late, too late, sērō, *adv.*

latter, hic, haec, hoc, *dem. pron.*

law, lex, lēgis, 3 *f.*, *or* iūs, iūris, 3 *n.*

lay waste (I), vasto, 1 *v. a.*

lead (I), dūco, -ere, -xi, -ctum, 3 *v. a.*; praesum, -esse, -fui, *v. n.* (*with dat.*).

lead back (I), redūco, -ere, -xi, -ctum, 3 v. a.

leader, dux, ducis, 3 m.

learned, doctus, -a, -um, adj.

leave (I), exeo, -īre, -ii, -itum, v. n. (with prep. ex, out of, or dē, down from).

left, sinister, -tra, -trum, adj.

left-hand, sinistra, -ae, 1 f. ; to the left, ad sinistram.

legion, legio, -ōnis, 3 f.

lend (I), praebeo, 2 v. a. ; as I lend help, praebeo auxilium.

less, minus, comp. adv.

letter, littera, -ae, 1 f. (of alphabet) ; litterae, -ārum, 1 f. pl., or epistola, -ae, 1 f. (epistle).

letter-carrier, tabellārius, -i, 2 m.

level (I), aequo, 1 v. a. ; to level with the ground, aequare sŏlo.

lie (I), iaceo, 2 v. n.

life, vīta, -ae, 1 f.

light (I), accendo, -ere, -di, -sum, 3 v. a.

limb, membrum, -i, 2 n.

listen (I), audio, 4 v. a.

little, parvus, -a, -um, adj.

little (a or too), parum, adv.

little (for a), paulisper, adv.

little (a little-away-from), paululum, adv. (with prep. ā).

live (I), habito, 1 v. a. (I dwell) ; vīvo, -ere, -xi, -ctum, 3 v. n. (I am alive).

lo, ecce, adv.

load (I), cumulo, 1 v. a. (I load with honours), or onero, 1 v. a. (I burden).

long, longus, -a, -um, adj.

long (for a long time), diū, adv.

longer, diūtius, adv.

longer (no), non iam.

look after (I), cūro, 1 v. a.

look at (I), specto, 1 v. a.

love, amor, -ōris, 3 m.

love (I), amo, 1 v. a.

Lucrine, Lŭcrīnus, -a, -um, adj.

luxury, luxuria, -ae, 1 f.

lyre, fides, -ium, 3 f. pl. ; I sing to the lyre, fidibus canto.

magistrate, magistrātus, -ūs, 4 m.

make (I), facio, -ere, fēci, factum, 3 v. a.

man, homo, -inis, 3 m. (male being) ; or vir, viri, 2 m. (hero).

many, multus, -a, -um, adj.

Marathon (of), Marathōnius, -a, -um, adj.

marble (of), marmoreus, -a, -um, adj.

March, Martius, -i, 2 m.

Marius, Marius, -i, 2 m.

mark (it is a mark of), est, with gen. of pers.

mark out (I), dēsigno, 1 v. a.

Mars, Mars, Martis, 3 m.

marsh, palūs, -ūdis, 3 f.

master, dominus, -i, 2 m. (a lord or host) ; magister, -tri, 2 m. (teacher, director).

match (a match for), pār, paris, adj. (with dat.).

matter, rēs, reī, 5 f.

Mausolus, Mausōlus, -i, 2 m.

meet (I), obviam eo, īre, īvi or ii, itum, v. n. (with dat. of pers.).

memory, memoria, -ae, 1 f. ;

I keep or **hold in memory,** memoriā teneo.

mention, memoria, -ae, 1 *f.* or recordātio, -ōnis, 3 *f.*

mighty, magnus, -a, -um, *adj.* or ingens, -entis, *adj.*

mind, mens, mentis, 3 *f.* (intellect); animus, -ī, 2 *m.* (heart).

mineral-waters, aquae, -ārum, 1 *f. pl.*

Minos, Mīnos, -ōis, 3 *m.*

mix (I), misceo, -ēre, miscui, mixtum, 2 *v. a.*

moderation, tem▮▮▮▮ia, -ae, 1 *f.*

money, pecūnia, -ae, 1 *f.*

month, mensis, -is, 3 *m.*

monument, monumentum, -ī, 2 *n.*

more (rather), magis, *comp. adv.* (*of quality*).

more, plūs, plūris, *neut. comp. adj.* (*of quantity*).

more highly, plūris (*gen. of price*).

mortal, mortālis, -e, *adj.*

mortal (a), homo, -inis, 3 *m. and f.*

most, *sign of superlative adjective.*

most, plūrimus, -a, -um, *sup. adj.*

move (I), moveo, -ēre, mōvi, mōtum, 2 *v. a.*

move (I move with anger), concito or incito, 1 *v. a.*

much, multum, *adv.*

music, mūsica, -ōrum, 2 *n. pl.*

my, meus, -a, -um (*voc.,* mi), *poss. adj.*

myself (I), ipse, ipsa, ipsum, *pron.*

name, nōmen, -minis, 3 *n.*

Naples, Neāpolis, -is, 3 *f.* (a▮ -im, *abl.* -i).

native-land, pătria, -ae, 1 *f.*

nature, nātūra, -ae, 1 *f.* ; it the nature of, ēst (*wi▮ gen. of pers.*).

near, prope, *prep.* (*with acc.*).

nearly, ferē or paene, *adv.*

necessary, necesse, *indec▮ adj.*

neglect (I), neglego, -ere, -x▮ -ctum, 3 *v. a.*

neither . . . nor, neque . . . ne▮ que (*before vowels*), or ne▮ . . . nec (*before consonants)*

never, nunquam, *adv.*

new, novus, -a, -um, *adj.*

night, nox, noctis, 3 *f.*

nine, novem, *num. adj.*

ninth, nōnus, -a, -um, *ord▮ adj.*

no, nullus, -a, -um, *adj.* (*gen▮ nullīus, dat.* nullī).

no (nothing), nihil, *indecl. subst. with part. gen., as* nihil pecuniae, no money.

no longer, non iam.

no one, nēmo, *acc.* nēminem, *dat.* nēmini ; *gen.* nullīus, *abl.* nullo, nulla.

noble, nōbilis, -e, *adj.*

nobody, *see* no one.

noise, strepitus, -ūs, 4 *m.*

nor, neque (*usually before vowels*), or nec.

not, nōn.

not ? nonne ?

not yet, nondum, *adv.*

nothing, nihil, *neut. indecl. subst.*

November, November, -bris, 3 *m.*

now, iam (*of time*); nunc (*of circumstances*).

now (since), quoniam, *conj.*

number, numerus, -i, 2 *m.*

obey (I), pāreo, 2 *v. n.* (*with dat.*), oboedio, 4 *v. n.* (*with dat.*).

object, res, reī, 5 *f.*; *sign of pred. dat., as* dēdecori, an object-of-disgrace.

ocean, ōceanus, -i, 2 *m.*

October, Octōber, -bris, 3 *m.*

of (about), dē, *prep. with abl.*

offend, offendo, -ere, -di, -sum, 3 *v. a.*

often, saepe, *adv.*

old, antīquus, -a, -um, *adj.* (ancient), vetulus, -a, -um, *adj.* (little old).

old-woman, vetula, -ae, 1 *f.*

olive, olīva, -ae, 1 *f.*

Olympian, Olympius, -a, -um, *adj.*

on, in, *prep. with abl.* (*to express place*); on (*to express cause or time*), *simple ablative.*

on account of, ob *or* propter, *prep.* (*with acc.*).

one, ūnus, -a, -um (*gen.* ūnīus, *dat.* ūnī), *num. adj.*

one (one . . . another), alius . . . alius.

one (the one . . . the other), alter . . . alter.

one hundred, centum, *num. adj.*

only, modo *or* sōlum, *adv.*

open *or* open up (I), aperio, -īre, -erui, -ertum, 4 *v. a.*

opportunity, occāsio, -ōnis, 3 *f.*

oppress (I), premo, -ere, pressi, pressum *or* opprimo, -ere, -pressi, -pressum, 3 *v. a.*

or, aut (*excludes one object*), vel (*gives a choice*).

orator, ōrātor, -ōris, 3 *m.*

other (the), alter, -era, -erum, *adj.*

others, alii; some . . . others, alii . . . alii.

others (the), cēteri, -ae, -a, *adj.*

our *or* ours, noster, -tra, -trum, *poss. pron.*

out of, ex, *prep.* (*with abl.*).

overcome, supero, 1 *v. a.*

overthrow, adflīgo, -ere, -flixi, -flictum, 3 *v. a.*

overwhelm (I), premo, -ere, pressi, pressum, *or* opprimo, -ere, -pressi, -pressum, 3 *v. a.*

oyster, ostrea, -ae, 1 *f.*

pace, passus, -ūs, 4 *m.*; mille passūs, a thousand paces (a Roman mile).

paint (I), pingo, -ere, pinxi, pictum, 3 *v. a.*

pardon, venia, -ae, 1 *f.*

pardon (I), veniam do.

patient, patiens, -entis, *adj.*

payment (without), grātīs, *adv.*

pay (I pay penalty), poenas do.

peace, pāx, pācis, 3 *f.*

people, populus, -i, 2 *m.*

Persian, Persicus, -a, -um, *adj.*

Pharsalian, Pharsālius, -a, -um, *adj.*

Phidias, Phīdias, -ae, 1 *m.*

Philip, Philippus, -i, 2 *m.*

philosopher, philosophus, -i, 2 *m.*

picture, tabula, -ae, 1 *f.*

place, locus, -i, 2 *m.* ; *plur.,* loci, *m.,* or loca, *n.*

place (I), colloco, 1 *v. a.*

place (I place confidence), fidem habeo (*with dat. of pers.*).

place (in place of), loco (*with gen.*).

plain, campus, -i, 2 *m.*

plan, consilium, -i, 2 *n.*

Plataea, Plataeae, -ārum, 1 *f. pl.*

Plato, Plato, -ōnis, 3 *m.*

pleasant, iūcundus, -a, -um, *adj.*

please (I), placeo, 2 *v. n.* (*with dat. of pers.*).

pleasing, grātus, -a, -um, *adj.*

pleasure, voluptas, -ātis, 3 *f.*

plotting, coniūrātio, -ōnis, 3 *f.* or insidiae, -ārum, 1 *f. pl.* (an ambush).

plough, arātrum, -i, 2 *n.*

plough (I), aro, 1 *v. a.*

poem, carmen, -minis, 3 *n.*

poet, poēta, -ae, 1 *m.*

Pompeii, Pompēii, -ōrum, 2 *m. pl.*

Pompey, Pompēius, -i, 2 *m.*

power, potestas, -ātis, 3 *f.,* or imperium, -i, 2 *n.*

powerful, magnus, -a, -um, *adj.,* or potens, -entis, *adj.*

powerful (I am), valeo, 2 *v. n.*

praise, laus, laudis, 3 *f.*

praise (I), laudo, 1 *v. a.*

preceptor, paedagōgus, -i, 2 *m.*

prefer (I), mālo, malle, mālui, *v. n.*

prepare (I), paro, 1 *v. a.*

present (I am), adsum, -esse, -fui, *v. n.*

preserve (I), servo, 1 *v. a.*

prevent (I), prohibeo, 2 *v.* (*with prep.* ā or ab from)

price, pretium, -ii, 2 *n.*

pride, superbia, -ae, 1 *f.*

prince, princeps, -cipis, 3 *m.*

protection, praesidium, -i, 2 *n.*

provide (I), praebeo, 2 *v. a.*

prudent, prūdens, -entis, *adj.*

Punic, Pūnicus, -a, -um, *adj.*

punish (I), castīgo, 1 *v. a.* (chastise); pūnio, 4 *v. a.*

punishment, poena, -ae, 1 *f.*

pupil, discipulus, -i, 2 *m.*

put, put-an-end-to (I) (fīnem) impōno, -ere, -posui, -positum, 3 *v. a.* (*with dat. of thing ended*).

put-to-flight (I), fugo, 1 *v. a.*

Puteoli, Puteoli, -ōrum, 2 *m. pl.*

quarrel, contentio, -ōnis, 3 *f.*

queen, rēgīna, -ae, 1 *f.*

quick, celer, celeris, celere, *adj.*

rage, īra, īrae, 1 *f.*

raise (I), struo, -ere, -xi, -ctum, 3 *v. a.* (*of a building*).

reach (I), adeo, -īre, -ii, -itum, *v. n.* (*with prep.* ad).

read (I), lego, -ere, lēgi, lectum, 3 *v. a.*

ready (I get), expedio, 4 *v. a.*

reason, causa, -ae, 1 *f.*

recall (I), recordor, -āri, -ātus sum, 1 *v. dep.*

receive (I), accipio, -ere, -cēpi, -ceptum, 3 *v. a.*

recite (I), recito, 1 *v. a.*

recline (I), accumbo, -ere, -cubui, -cubitum, 3 *v. n.* (*at table*).

recollection, memoria, -ae, 1 *f.*

refuse (I), nego, 1 *v. a.*

reject (I), repudio, 1 *v. a.*

rejoice (I), gaudeo, -ēre, gāvī-sus sum, 2 *v. n.*

relate (I), narro, 1 *v. a.* (*with* dē, about, *and abl.*).

release (I), lībero, 1 *v. a.* (*with simple abl.*).

remain (I), maneo, -ēre, mansi, mansum, 2 *v. n.* ; super-sum, -esse, -fui (**survive**).

remove (I), removeo, -ēre, -mōvi, -mōtum, 2 *v. a.*

renew (I), renovo, 1 *v. a.*

report (I), nuntio, 1 *v. a.*

republic, rēs publica, *gen.*, rei publicae.

return (I), redeo, -īre, -ii, -itum, *v. n.*

revere (I), veneror, -āri, -ātus sum, 1 *v. dep.*

reward, praemium, -i, 2 *n.*

riches, dīvitiae, -ārum, 1 *f. pl.*

right, dexter, -tera, -terum, *or* dexter, -tra, -trum, *adj.*

right-hand, dextera, -ae, *or* dextra, -ae, 1 *f.*

robber, lătro, -ōnis, 3 *m.*

rock, saxum, -i, 2 *n.*

Roman, Rōmānus, -a, -um, *adj.*

Rome, Rōma, -ae, 1 *f.*

rouse (I), excito, 1 *v. a.*, *or* excio, 4 *v. a.* (*with prep.* ex).

rout (I), fugo, 1 *v. a.*

rule (I), rego, -ere, -xi, -ctum, 3 *v. a.*

rule, rēgula, -ae, 1 *f.*

rustic, rusticus, -a, -um, *adj.*

sacred, sacer, -cra, -crum, *adj.*

sacrifice (I), macto, 1 *v. a.*

sad, tristis, -e, *or* maestus, -a, -um, *adj.*

safety, salūs, -ūtis, 3 *f.*

sail (I), nāvigo, 1 *v. n.* (*with prep.* in *or* ad *and acc.*).

sailor, nauta, -ae, 1 *f.*

same, īdem, eadem, idem, *pron.*

sandal, solea, -ae, 1 *f.*

save (I), servo, 1 *v. a.* (*with prep.* ex *and abl.*).

say (I), dīco, -ere, -xi, -ctum, 3 *v. a.*

scarcely, vix, *adv.*

school, lūdus, -i, 2 *m.* (*for children*); schola, -ae, 1 *f.* (*school of philosophy*).

Scipio, Scīpio, -ōnis, 3 *m.*

Scythian, Scytha, -ae, 1 *m.*

sea, mare, maris, 3 *n.*

season, tempus, -poris, 3 *n.*

second, secundus, -a, -um, *adj.*; alter, -era, -erum, *adj.* (*of two things*).

see (I), video, -ēre, vīdi, vīsum, 2 *v. a.*

seem (I), videor, -ēri, vīsus sum, 2 *v. dep. and pass.*

senate, senātus, -ūs, 4 *m.*

senators, pătres, pătrum, 3 *m. pl.*

send (I), mitto, -ere, mīsi, missum, 3 *v. a.*

sense, sensus, -ūs, 4 *m.*

September, September, -bris, 3 *m.*

seriously, graviter, *adv.*

set (I set an example), ex-emplum do.

set out (I), proficiscor, -i, pro-fectus sum, 3 *v. dep.*

settle (I), colloco, 1 *v. a.*

seven, septem, *num. adj.*

seven hundred, septingenti, -ae, -a, *num. adj.*

seventh, septimus, -a, -um, *ord. adj.*

severe, gravis, -e, *adj.*

severely, graviter, *adv.*

shade, umbra, -ae, 1 *f.*

Shades, Mānēs, -ium, 3 *m. pl.*

share (I), partior, -īri, -ītus sum, 4 *v. dep.*

sheep, ovis, -is, 3 *f.*

ship, nāvis, -is, 3 *f.*

shore, lītus, -oris, 3 *n.*

shout (I), clāmo, 1 *v. a.*

shout, clāmor, -ōris, 3 *m.*

show (I), monstro, 1 *v. a.* (*with dat. of pers.*); I show zeal, studium praebeo.

Sicily, Sicilia, -ae, 1 *f.*

simple, humilis, -e, *adj.*

sin (I), pecco, 1 *v. n.*

sing (I), canto, 1 *v. a. and n.*, or cano, -ere, cecini, cantum, 3 *v. a. and n.*

six, sex, *num. adj.*

sixteen, sēdecim, *num. adj.*

skin, pellis, -is, 3 *f.*

slaughter, caedes, -is, 3 *f.*

slave, servus, -i, 2 *m.*

sleep, somnus, -i, 2 *m.*

small, parvus, -a, -um, *adj.*

smaller, minor, -us, *comp. adj.*

smallest, minimus, -a, -um, *sup. adj.*

so, sīc *or* ita, *adv.*

so long, tam diū, *adv.* ; tam longus, *adj.*

Socrates, Sōcrates, -is, 3 *m.*

soldier, mīles, -itis, 3 *m.*

Solon, Solōn, -ōnis, 3 *m.*

some ... others, alii ... alii.

son, fīlius, -i, 2 *m.*

song, carmen, -inis, 3 *n.*

soon, mox, *adv.*

sorrow, dolor, -ōris, 3 *m.*

sorry (I am), doleo, 2 *v. n.* (*with* quod, *conj.*, because *or* that).

source, *sign of pred. dat., as,* a source of care, cūrae.

Spain, Hispānia, -ae, 1 *f.*

speak (I), dīco, -ere, dixi, dictum, 3 *v. a.* ; loquor, loqui, locūtus sum, 3 *v. dep.*

speech, ōrātio, -ōnis, 3 *f.*

spend (I), ago, -ere, ēgi, actum, 3 *v. a.* (*of time or life*).

spirit, animus, -i, 2 *m.*

splendid, splendidus, -a, -um, *adj.*

spring, vēr, vēris, 3 *n.*

stand, sto, stāre, steti, statum, 1 *v. n.*

start (I), commoveo, -ēre, -mōvi, -mōtum, 2 *v. a.* (*of a war*).

state, cīvitas, -ātis, 3 *f.*

statue, statua, -ae, 1 *f.* ; signum, -i, 2 *n.*

stay (I), maneo, -ēre, mansi, mansum, 2 *n.*

still, adhūc, *adv.*

stone, saxum, -i, 2 *n.*

stop (I), impedio, 4 *v. a.*

storm (I), expugno, 1 *v. a.*

story, fābula, -ae, 1 *f.*

stranger, advena, -ae, 1 *m.*

strategy, ars, artis, 3 *f.*

strength, firmitas, -ātis, 3 *f.* ; vīres, vīrium, 3 *f. pl.*

strengthen (I), firmo, 1 *v. a.*

strict, sevērus, -a, -um, *adj.*

strike (I), pulso, 1 *v. a.*

strive (I), nītor, nīti, nīsus *or* nixus sum, 3 *v. dep.*

study, studium, -ii, 2 *n.*

suffer (I), patior, pati, passus sum, 3 *v. dep.*

sufficient, satis, *indecl. adj.*

suitable, aptus, -a, -um, *adj.*

summer, aestas, -ātis, 3 *f.*

sun, sōl, sōlis, 3 *m.*

superior, superior, -us, *comp. adj.*

surely, nempe, *adv.*

surpass (I), supero, 1 *v. a.* (*with abl. of thing in which one is surpassed*).

surround (I), cingo, -ere, cinxi, cinctum, 3 *v. a.*

sweet, dulcis, -e, *adj.*

sword, gladius, -ii, 2 *m.*

table, mensa, -ae, 1 *f.*

take (I), teneo, -ēre, tenui, tentum, 2 *v. a.* (*hold*).

take away (I), dēmo, -ere, dempsi, demptum, 3 *v. a.*

take care (I), caveo, -ēre, cāvi, cautum, 2 *v. a. and n.*

take up (I), capio, -ēre, cēpi, captum, 3 *v. a.*; arma capio, I take up arms.

tale, fābula, -ae, 1 *f.*

task, opus, -eris, 3 *n.*

teach (I), doceo, -ēre, docui, doctum, 2 *v. a.*

tell (I), dīco, -ere, dixi, dictum, 3 *v. a.*

tell a story (I), recito, 1 *v. a.*

temple, templum, -i, 2 *n.*

tempt (I), sollicito, 1 *v. a.*

ten, decem, *num. adj.*

tenth, decimus, -a, -um, *ord. adj.*

terms, condicio, -ōnis, 3 *f.*

terrify (I), terreo, 2 *v. a.*; per-terreo, 2 *v. a.*

Teutons, Teutoni, -ōrum, 2 *m. pl.*

than (*after a comparative*), quam, *followed by the same case as precedes; or by abla-tive alone, if the preceding case is a nom. or acc.*

thanks, grātia, -ae, 1 *f.* (*used in plural if the verb is ago*).

that, is, ea, id; *or* ille, illa, illud, *dem. pron.*

that, *conj., see* because.

that which, id quod.

thee, *see* thou.

their, their own (*reflex.*), suus, -a, -um, *poss. pron.*

their (*not reflex.*), eorum, earum (*gen. of* is, ea, id).

them, *oblique cases plural of* is, ea, id.

themselves, sē *or* sēsē, *reflex. pron.*

themselves, (they), ipsi, -ae, -a, *pron.*

then, tum, *adv.*

there, ibĭ, *adv.*; there is, est; can there be? num potest esse?; who is there? quis adest?

these, hī, hae, haec, *plur. of* hic.

thing, rēs, rei, 5 *f.*

think (I), puto, 1 *v. a.*

third, tertius, -a, -um, *ord. adj.*

thirty, trīgintā, *num. adj.*

this, hīc, haec, hōc, *dem. pron.*

those, ei, eae, ea, *plur. of* is; *or* illi, illae, illa, *plur. of* ille.

thou, tū, 2 *pers. pron.*

thousand, mille (*num. adj.*); *in plur.,* mīlia (*subst.*).

three, trēs, tria, *num. adj.*

threshold, līmen, -inis, 3 *n.*

through, per, *prep.* (*with acc.*).

through, *sign of abl. of cause,* as, timōre, through fear.

throw (I), iacio, -ere, iēci, iactum, 3 *v. a.*

thus, sīc, *adv.*

thy, tuus, -a, -um, *poss. adj.*

tide, aestus, -ūs, 4 *m.*

time, tempus, -oris, 3 *n.* ; in-time, tempore, *or* ad tempus.

time (for a long), diū, *adv.*

timid, timidus, -a, -um, *adj.*

tire (I), dēfatīgo, 1 *v. a.*

tired, dēfatīgātus, -a, -um, *or* fessus, -a, -um, *adj.*

to, *prep. of motion,* ad *or* in *with acc.* (ad *meaning* toward *or* up to ; in *meaning* into).

to-day, hodiē, *adv.*

tomb, sepulcrum, -i, 2 *n.*

too little, parum, *adv.*

too much, nimis, *adv.*

torture (I), crucio, 1 *v. a.*

town, oppidum, -i, 2 *n.* (*of towns other than Rome, which was called* urbs).

train (I), ērudio, 4 *v. a.*

tree, arbor, -boris, 3 *f.*

tribe, nātio, -ōnis, 3 *f.*

triclinium, trīclīnium, -i, 2 *n.*

Trojan, Trōiānus, -a, -um, *adj.*

true, vērus, -a, -um, *adj.*

trust (I), fīdo, -ere, fīsus sum, 3 *v. n.*, *or* confīdo, -ere, -fīsus sum, 3 *v. n.* (*with dat. of pers.*).

twelfth, duodecimus, -a, -um, *ord. num.*

twelve, duodecim, *num. adj.*

twelve hundred, mille ducenti, -ae, -a, *num. adj.*

twenty, vīgintī, *num. adj.*

two, duo, duae, duo, *num. adj.*

two hundred, ducenti, -ae, -a, *num. adj.*

tyrant, tyrannus, -i, 2 *m.*

Tyrians, Tyrii, -ōrum, 2 *m. pl.*

Ulysses, Ulīxes, -is, 3 *m.*

uncertain, incertus, -a, -um, *adj.*

under, sub, *prep.* (*with abl.*).

undertake (I), comparo, 1 *v. a.* (*of a journey*).

ungrateful, ingrātus, -a, -um, *adj.*

unless, nisi, *conj.*

unsuccessful, adversus, -a, -um, *adj.* ; infēlix, -līcis, *adj.*

unwilling (I am), nōlo, nolle, nōlui, *v. n. irreg.*

upon, in, *prep.* (*with acc.*).

urge on (I), incito, 1 *v. a.*

us, nōs, 1 *pers. pron. pl.*

used, *sign of imperfect tense.*

useful, ūtilis, -e, *adj.*

vain, vānus, -a, -um, *adj.*

vain (in), frustrā, *adv.*

value (I), aestimo, 1 *v. a.* ; *with gen. of price,* magni, highly ; plūris, more highly.

very, multum, *adv.* (very *is also a sign of the superlative*).

very great, maximus, -a, -um, *sup. adj.*

very large, *see* very great.

very many, plūrimus, -a, -um, *sup. adj.*

very much, plūrimum, *sup. adv.*

Vesta, Vesta, -ae, 1 *f.*

vice, vitium, -ii, 2 *n.*

victorious, victor, -ōris, *m.* ; victrix, -īcis, *f.*, *adj.*

victory, victōria, -ae, 1 *f.* ; I gain a victory over, victōriam reporto ā *or* ab (*with abl. of pers.*).

virtue, virtūs, -ūtis, 3 *f.*

visit (I), vīso, -ere, vīsi, visum, 3 *v. a.*

visit (I) (with wounds, punishment, &c.), afficio, -ere, -fēci, -fectum, 3 *v. a.*

wage (I), gero, -ere, gessi, gestum, 3 *v. a.*

wait for (I), exspecto, 1 *v. a.*

walls (town), moenia, -ium, 3 *n. pl.*

wander (I), erro, 1 *v. n.* (*with prep. ā or* ex).

want (I), opto, 1 *v. a.* ; dēsīdero, 1 *v. a.*

war, bellum, -i, 2 *n.*

warn, moneo, 2 *v. a.*

wave, fluctus, -ūs, 4 *m.*

way, via, viae, 1 *f.*

we, nōs, 1 *pers. pron. plur.*

wealth, dīvitiae, -ārum, 1 *f. pl.*

weapon, tēlum, -i, 2 *n.*

wear out (I), dēfatīgo, 1 *v. a.*

well, bene, *adv.*

what, quid, *interrog. pron.*

what, qui, quae, quod (*interrog. adj. used with noun*).

what (that which), id quod.

when, quandō, *interrog. adv.*

when, ubī, *adv.*

whence, unde, *adv.*

where, ubī, *adv.*

which, qui, quae, quod, *rel. or interrog. pron.*

while, dum, *conj.* (*with pres. indic.*).

whither, quō, *interrog. adv.*

who, qui, quae, quod, *rel. pron.* ; quis, quis, quid, *interrog. pron.*

why, cūr, *interrog. adv.*

wicked, malus, -a, -um, *adj.*, *or* improbus, -a, -um, *adj.*

wife, uxor, -ōris, 3 *f.*

willing (I am), volo, velle, volui, *v. a. irreg.*

win (I), reporto, 1 *v. a.*

wind, ventus, -i, 2 *m.*

wine, vīnum, -i, 2 *n.*

winter, hiems, -emis, 3 *f.*

wisdom, sapientia, -ae, 1 *f.*

wise, sapiens, -entis, *adj.*

wish (I), opto, 1 *v. a.*, *or* volo, velle, volui, *v. a. irreg.*

with, cum, *prep. with abl.* (*joined after personal and relative pronouns, as* mēcum, tēcum, quōcum, *&c.*).

with difficulty, aegrē, *adv.*

without, sine, *prep.* (*with abl.*).

without payment, grātīs, *adv.*

witty, facētus, -a, -um, *adj.*

woman, fēmina, -ae, 1 *f.* ; old woman, vetula, -ae, 1 *f.*

wonder, mīrāculum, -i, 2 *n.*

wood, silva, -ae, 1 *f.*

word, verbum, -i, 2 *n.*

work, labor, -ōris, 3 *m.* (labour); opus, -eris (result of labour), 3 *n.*

work (I), labōro, 1 *v. n.*

world, mundus, -i, 2 *m.* ; orbis terrarum *or* orbis, -is, 3 *m.*

worn out, dēfatīgātus, -a, -um, *adj.*

worthy, dignus, -a, -um, *adj.* (*with abl.*).

wound, vulnus, -eris, 3 *n.*

wretched, miser, -era, -erum, *adj.*

write, scrĭbo, -ere, scripsi, scriptum, 3 *v. a.*

writing, scriptum, -i, 2 *n.*

wrong (I), violo, 1 *v. a.*

year, annus, -i, 2 *m.*

yet, tamen, *adv.* (*cannot stand first*).

you, tū, 2 *pers. pron.*

your, tuus, -a, -um (*of one pers.*). or vester, -tra, -trum (*of more than one person*), *poss. pron.*

yourself, tē, *pers. pron.*

yourselves, vōs, *pers. pron.*

youth, iuventus, -ūtis, 3 *f.*

BELL'S ILLUSTRATED CLASSICS

Latin Course, Latin Readers and First Greek Reader

EDITED BY E. C. MARCHANT, M.A.

FELLOW OF LINCOLN COLLEGE, OXFORD
AND LATE CLASSICAL MASTER AT ST. PAUL'S SCHOOL

'The testimony of many scholars to their excellence should suffice to give the *Series* an introduction to the best preparatory schools. They are exactly such as will interest and instruct the young learner of Latin. The illustrations appeal to the eye and fix themselves firmly in the memory.'—*School Guardian.*

LONDON
GEORGE BELL & SONS, YORK STREET, COVENT GARDEN.

Bell's Illustrated Latin Readers.

Uniform with the ILLUSTRATED CLASSICS.

Price One Shilling each.

>———→•←———

SCALAE PRIMAE. Simple Stories for Translation, with Notes and Vocabulary. By J. G. SPENCER, B.A., St. Paul's Preparatory School. With Twenty-nine Illustrations.

SCALAE MEDIAE. Extracts from Eutropius and Caesar. With Notes and Vocabulary. By PERCY A. UNDERHILL, M.A. With Twenty Illustrations.

SCALAE TERTIAE. Graduated Extracts in Verse and Prose from Phaedrus, Ovid, Nepos, and Cicero. With Notes and Vocabulary. By E. C. MARCHANT, M.A. With Twenty-eight Illustrations.

'A better book for use in Secondary Schools could not be procured.'—*Educational News.*

'Well-arranged Readers, containing interesting selections and alluring pictures.'—*Cambridge Review.*

'No intelligent boy can fail to be interested as well as instructed by the use of such books. The whole series is worthy of the highest praise.'—*School Guardian.*

>———→•←———

Crown 8vo, with Thirty Illustrations. 1s. 6d

ΚΛΙΜΑΞ ΠΡΩΤΗ.

A FIRST GREEK READER.

In Two Progressive Parts. With Hints & Vocabulary.

By E. C. MARCHANT, M.A.

'This attractive little book is the analogue of the same publishers' "Scalae Primae." Mr. Marchant rightly takes his young pupils at a faster rate than is possible in Latin. With the illustrations in the text the budding Grecians who are lucky enough to use this booklet should find their first year in Greek pleasant going.'—*Athenaeum.*

In Three Parts. With Coloured Plates and numerous other Illustrations. Price 1s. 6d. each.

BELL'S LATIN COURSE

FOR THE FIRST YEAR.

BY

E. C. MARCHANT, M.A., AND J. G. SPENCER, B.A.

THIS Latin Course is intended to be used for the instruction of children who have not hitherto done any Latin. The Course is complete in itself, and may be used without the aid of dictionary or grammar.

Believing that the elementary teaching of Latin has made more advance on the Continent than in England, the authors have examined the most successful German works on the subject. They have also sought the advice of leading authorities on Education, both English and American; and it is hoped that their method will commend itself to training colleges as well as to preparatory schools.

'For an elementary reading or exercise book two things are requisite. Each section should deal mainly with a single difficulty, and each should be worth reading for its own sake. Both conditions are fulfilled in this book, and its value is increased by the excellent illustrations from the antique. . . . Altogether it is one of the most successful attempts at "Latin without tears" which have come under our notice.'—*Educational Times.*

'If learning the elements of Latin can be made attractive to small boys, Messrs. Marchant and Spencer have discovered the method. We commend the Course to the attention of all who are teaching the young idea how to shoot. A book so simple, so natural, and so attractive is sure to catch on. Latin at last becomes a delight. Four coloured plates and twenty-seven other illustrations adorn the volume. Other characteristics of the compilation are—rules following (instead of preceding) the exercises, so as to sum up what has been learnt in the exercise; and learning by means of picture and type, the vocabulary being picked up by picture practice.'—*School Guardian.*

'We hope that no one will suppose that because an attractive appearance is given and much use is made of pictures, therefore the work may be called childish. It is a genuine attempt to teach Latin *secundam naturam*, and as such merits our strongest approval. As the authors say, "*ridentem dicere verum quid vetat?* is a question to which in teaching children it is safe and right to answer '*nihil*'." They justifiably add: "We determined to admit nothing into this book that is not real Latin".'—*Secondary Education.*

'We have never seen a book containing so near an approach to a "royal road" of learning Latin as is displayed in this volume.'—*Educational News.*

'One of the best primers of the sort we have ever seen. It makes the learning of Latin positively a pleasure, and by easy and simple processes takes the scholar forward and ensures his progress. The system adopted is admirable, and there would be few tears shed by little pupils if this Latin Course were adopted in schools, as it deserves to be.'—*Birmingham Daily Gazette.*

'An attractive book of well-graded lessons for the use of beginners in Latin, adorned by many interesing illustrations, some of which are coloured. The book is skilfully devised not only to teach a youngster the elements of Latin, but to win him naturally to an interest in the subject.'—*Scotsman.*

3

BELL'S ILLUSTRATED CLASSICS.

THE special object of the Series is to make the editions as interesting and helpful as possible to the intelligent learner; and, with this object, numerous **Illustrations** *have been introduced. These are gathered from the best sources, and are chosen with a view to explaining the text, and making the reader more familiar with Greek and Roman life.*

Maps *and* **Plans** *are also inserted wherever they are required.*

The volumes are equipped with Introductions, Notes, Grammatical Appendices, and in some of the prose authors, Exercises on the Text. Vocabularies are also given, but the volumes may be had without the Vocabularies, if preferred.

The volumes are printed at the Oxford University Press, pott 8vo, and are issued, **with or without Vocabularies,** *at* **1s. 6d.** *each, except the Greek Plays, which are* **2s.** *each.*

'The introductions and explanatory matter are to the full as good and satisfactory as in rival editions, while the illustrations are well fitted to give youth more vivid conceptions of ancient life and thought than can be gathered from any amount of literary description—at least such description they will very usefully supplement. The photographic camera and all the museums of Europe have contributed their quota to these illustrations, which have the additional merit of really beautiful execution. The books, moreover, are handy in form, and for the higher schoolboy or the undergraduate they are hard to beat.'—*Glasgow Herald.*

'The master of junior forms and preparatory schools should make the acquaintance of this Series of Illustrated Classics; it surpasses all we have seen.'—*School Guardian.*

'Of all the five volumes which are before us it may be said that the illustrations are excellent, and that no expense has been spared to make the Series a success. The notes are mostly simple, and to the point. The introductions are clear and not "too full".'—*Cambridge Review.*

'The editors know their business, and the publishers have seconded their efforts in a most spirited fashion. The Series is sure to receive a welcome.'—*Educational Times.*

THE PLAUSTRUM. (From bas-reliefs.)

BELL'S ILLUSTRATED CLASSICS.

Elementary Series.

Pott 8vo, with or without Vocabularies, price 1s. 6d. each except the Greek Plays, which are 2s. each.

CAESAR. Book I. By A. C. LIDDELL, M.A., High School, Nottingham.

—— Book II. By A. C. LIDDELL, M.A.

—— Book III. By F. H. COLSON, M.A., Head Master of Plymouth College, and G. M. GWYTHER, M.A., Assistant Master.

—— Book IV. By Rev. A. W. UPCOTT, M.A., Head Master of Christ's Hospital.

—— Book V. By A. REYNOLDS, M.A., Merchant Taylors' School.

—— Book VI. By J. T. PHILLIPSON, M.A., Head Master of Christ's College, Finchley.

CICERO. Speeches against Catiline. I and II (1 vol.). By F. HERRING, M.A., Blundell's School, Tiverton.

—— **Selections.** By J. F. CHARLES, B.A., City of London School.

—— **De Senectute.** By A. S. WARMAN, B.A., Grammar School, Manchester.

—— **De Amicitia.** By H. J. L. J. MASSÉ, M.A., St. Paul's Preparatory School.

BELL'S ILLUSTRATED CLASSICS.

CORNELIUS NEPOS. Epaminondas, Hannibal, Cato. By H. I. EARL, M.A., Grammar School, Manchester.

EUTROPIUS. Books I and II (1 vol.). By J. G. SPENCER, B.A., St Paul's Preparatory School.

HORACE'S ODES. Book I. By C. G. BOTTING, B.A., St. Paul's School.

—— Book II. By C. G. BOTTING, B.A.

—— Book III. By H. LATTER, M.A., Cheltenham College.

—— Book IV. By H. LATTER, M.A.

LIVY. Book IX, cc. i–xix. By W. C. FLAMSTEAD WALTERS, M.A., Professor of Classics in King's College, London.

—— Hannibal's First Campaign in Italy. (Selected from Book XXI.) By F. E. A. TRAYES, M.A., St. Paul's School.

OVID'S METAMORPHOSES. Book I. By G. H. WELLS, M.A., Merchant Taylors' School.

—— Selection from the Metamorphoses. By J. W. E. PEARCE, M.A.

—— Elegiac Selections. By F. COVERLEY SMITH, B.A., High School, Nottingham.

—— Tristia. Book I. By A. E. ROGERS, M.A.

—— Tristia. Book III. By H. R. WOOLRYCH, M.A., Head Master of Blackheath School.

PHAEDRUS. A Selection. By Rev. R. H. CHAMBERS, M.A., Head Master of Christ's College, Brecon.

STORIES OF GREAT MEN. By Rev. F. CONWAY, M.A., Merchant Taylors' School.

VERGIL'S AENEID. Book I. By Rev. E. H. S. ESCOTT, M.A., Dulwich College.

—— Book II. By L. D. WAINWRIGHT, M.A., St. Paul's School.

—— Book III. By L. D. WAINWRIGHT, M.A.

—— Book IV. By A. S. WARMAN, B.A., Grammar School, Manchester.

—— Book V. By J. T. PHILLIPSON, M.A., Head Master of Christ's College, Finchley.

—— Book VI. By J. T. PHILLIPSON, M.A.

—— Selections from Books VII to XII. By W. G. COAST, M.A., Fettes College.

BELL'S ILLUSTRATED CLASSICS.

XENOPHON'S ANABASIS. Book I. By E. C. MARCHANT, M.A.

—— Book II. By E. C. MARCHANT, M.A.

—— Book III. By E. C. MARCHANT, M.A.   [*In the Press.*

GREEK PLAYS (2s. each).

AESCHYLUS' PROMETHEUS VINCTUS. By C. E. LAURENCE, M.A., Blackheath School.

EURIPIDES' ALCESTIS. By E. H. BLACKENEY, M.A., Head Master of Sir W. Borlase's School, Great Marlow. ·

—— **Bacchae.** By G. M. GWYTHER, M.A., Plymouth College.

—— **Hecuba.** By Rev. A. W. UPCOTT, M.A., Head Master of Christ's Hospital.

—— **Medea.** By Rev. T. NICKLIN, M.A., Rossall School.

Intermediate Series.

With numerous Illustrations and Maps. Crown 8vo.

CAESAR'S SEVENTH CAMPAIGN IN GAUL, B.C. 52. **De Bello Gallico.** Lib. VII. Edited, with Notes, Excursus, and Tables of Idioms, by the Rev. W. COOKWORTHY COMPTON, M.A., Head Master of Dover College. Fifth Edition. 2s. 6d. *net.*

LIVY. Book XXI. Edited by F. E. A. TRAYES, M.A., St. Paul's School. With numerous Illustrations, Maps, and Plans. 2s. 6d. *net.*

TACITUS: AGRICOLA. Edited by J. W. E. PEARCE, M.A., late Assistant Master at University College School. With numerous Illustrations and Map, 2s.

HOMER'S ODYSSEY. Book I. Edited by E. C. MARCHANT, M.A., late Classical Master of St. Paul's School. With numerous Illustrations. 2s.

SOPHOCLES' ANTIGONE. Edited by G. H. WELLS, M.A., Assistant Master at Merchant Taylors' School. With numerous Illustrations. 3s. 6d.

THE ATHENIANS IN SICILY. Being portions of Thucydides, Books VI and VII. Edited by the Rev. W. COOKWORTHY COMPTON, M.A., Head Master of Dover College. With numerous Illustrations and Maps. 3s. 6d.

# Some Opinions of Schoolmasters.

SELECTED FROM HUNDREDS OF TESTIMONIALS RECEIVED BY
THE PUBLISHERS.

'Our Senior Classical Master has thoroughly examined the volumes, and i much pleased with them. He speaks so well of them that I shall take an earl opportunity of introducing the series.'—W. P. WORKMAN, *Kingswood Schoo* *Bath.*

'Your "Illustrated Classics" seem to me excellent. I have already intro duced the "Caesar," and hope to use others.'—Rev. R. COLLEY, *Stonyhurs College, Blackburn.*

'It would be difficult to praise them too highly. They are really excellent.'— Dr. LATHAM, *Thornton Grammar School, Bradford.*

'Distinctly good of their kind. I shall consider their introduction favour ably when opportunity offers.'—Rev. H. B. GRAY, *Bradfield College.*

'I like them very much better, I think, than any I have previously seen.'— Rev. J. W. BECKETT, *Grammar School, Burton-on-Trent.*

'I am very favourably impressed with the "Illustrated Classics" that you have sent me. In every respect they seem admirably suited for use in the lower form of schools. I shall hope to make use of them in our school.'—G. G. PRUEN, *Cheltenham College.*

'It is impossible not to think most favourably of your "Illustrated Classics".'—W. WILKINS, *The High School, Dublin.*

'The illustrations seem to me good, and useful for rousing interest and increasing appreciation of the subject-matter. I have often in teaching wanted just such illustrations.'—Rev. Dr. WILSON, *Lancing College.*

'I have always been strongly in favour of the employment of illustration to assist the study of the classics. I am glad to see so definite an attempt to help us in this direction, and sincerely hope it will prove a success.'—Rev. Dr. FIELD, *Radley.*

'They seem to me clear and well done, and likely to attract boys more than the ordinary editions. I am distinctly pleased with them.'—Rev. E. J. W. HOUGHTON, *School House, Stratford-on-Avon.*

'The illustrations and the clear type are excellent features.'—J. H. FOWLER, *Clifton College.*

'I think your "Illustrated Classics" are the best on the market. The illustrations are most interesting and valuable.'—W. A. LISTER, *Corporation Grammar School, Grimsby.*

LONDON: GEORGE BELL & SONS.

OXFORD: PRINTED BY HORACE HART AT THE UNIVERSITY PRESS.

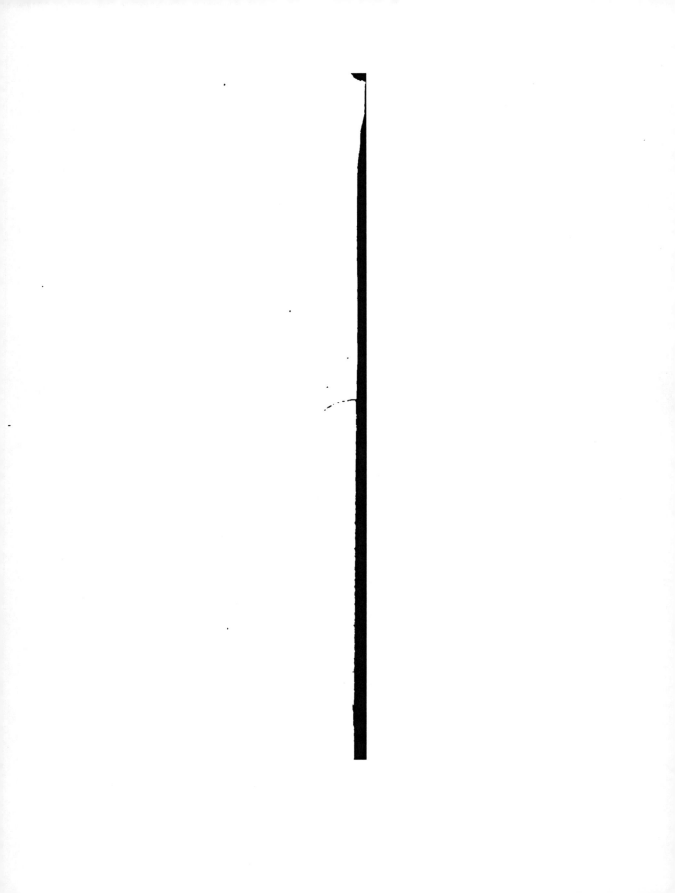

CPSIA information can be obtained at www.ICGtesting.com
Printed in the USA
BVOW07s1054130314

347556BV00007B/119/P